MW01492106

How to Talk About Jesus with Anyone

Tested Techniques for Planting Seeds and Saving Souls

Steve Dawson
with Cy Kellett

Catholic
Answers
Press

Published by Catholic Answers, Inc.
2020 Gillespie Way
El Cajon, California 92020
1-888-291-8000 orders
619-387-0042 fax
catholic.com

Printed in the United States of America

Cover design by eBookLaunch.com
Text layout by Shawna Kunz | Lime Design | shawna@limedesign.co

978-1-68357-400-2
978-1-68357-401-9 Kindle
978-1-68357-402-6 ePub

Dedication

To the Sacred Heart of Jesus and the Immaculate Heart of Mary—may this work bring you glory and draw many souls into the embrace of your mercy.

-Steve

To my children, Audrey, Sophie, and Graham.
Jesus loves you.

-Cy

But how are they to call on one in whom they have not believed?
And how are they to believe in one of whom they have never heard?
And how are they to hear without someone to proclaim him?
Romans 10:14-15

Contents

Introduction: On the Lookout 11

Part I: Know the Message 31

1. Know the Full and Balanced Gospel 33
2. Craft Your Personal Message 45

Part II: Share the Message 61

3. Adopt the Four-Step Method 63
4. Make Friends for Jesus 69
5. Learn to Listen 75
6. Open with Faith 83
7. Try Icebreakers 89
8. Hone the Skill of Friendship 97
9. Prepare Your Reasons 105
10. Give "One Good Reason" 111
11. Share the Promise *and* the Warning 117

Part III: Live the Message 125

12. Be Yourself Converted 127
13: Put on the Armor of God 137
14. Don't Quit! 151
15. Build Evangelizing Communities 157

Conclusion: Go and Make Disciples 167

Postscript:
An Invitation to St. Paul Street Evangelization 173

Acknowledgements

I would like to acknowledge my wife and best friend, Maria—our life together is my greatest earthly gift—as well as our children, along with our family, the Dawsons and the Michaliks, whose love and support have shaped and sustained me throughout my journey and the writing of this book. Likewise, my parents—whose faith, love, and prayers have marked my life profoundly.

Finally, let me acknowledge my team at St. Paul Street Evangelization. You inspire me every day with your faith, your courage, and your love for the lost.

-Steve

On the Lookout

So, you want to talk with people about Jesus.

Well, no need to run out and get yourself a bullhorn. You won't need it. Nor will you need any hand-painted signs about hell or the apocalypse. Also, you can leave your debate skills at home, for the most part.

Will you need a degree in theology?

No.

The holiness of a saint?

Nope.

How about a magnetic personality?

It probably couldn't hurt, but no need for charm school.

What about toughness? Do you need to be the kind of hard-shelled person who can handle lots of rejection and yelling and spite?

Actually, not so much. You'll almost certainly deal with less conflict than your average McDonald's worker.

The truth is this: if you have met Jesus, if you have received the sacraments, and if you now live the life of faith, you already have almost everything you need to talk with anyone about Jesus.

What more do you need? Consider the conversion of the apostle Paul:

> Now as he was going along and approaching Damascus, suddenly a light from heaven flashed around him. He fell

to the ground and heard a voice saying to him, "Saul, Saul, why do you persecute me?" He asked, "Who are you, Lord?" The reply came, "I am Jesus, whom you are persecuting. But get up and enter the city, and you will be told what you are to do" (Acts 9:3-6).

When Paul followed this command, he met the Church in Damascus and received the help of Ananias. Certainly, there he received instruction and formation.

Like Paul, we who have received Jesus need to "get up and enter the city" so that we can be told what to do. We need basic instruction, and we need the community and sacraments of the Church. But lots of us have already received these things. And if we have this basic formation, we have most of what we need to share Jesus with others.

All we might need in that case is the *confidence* that comes from having a bit of instruction in the best methods. In fact, seeking these methods is probably why you have this book in your hands. The good news is that for more than a century the leaders of the Church, especially popes, have been calling on Catholics to get out and share the good news. And, because many people have heeded these calls, there is a good amount of contemporary experience for us to draw on as we consider how to evangelize today. We also have what might be the greatest possible help in the example of the great missionary saints throughout the ages.

The gospel hasn't changed. It hasn't gotten more complicated or difficult to share in our lifetime. We just got out of

 Evangelization is not optional—it's the mandatory calling of every Catholic.

the habit of doing it! But the Church is re-learning the old evangelizing habits and being re-filled with the old evangelizing spirit. Countless ministries, programs, apostolates, and communities have heeded the call to share Jesus with modern people. What we share in this book flows from decades spent among these movements in the Church.

Proclaiming in a Wounded World

With all that in mind, the first thing to know about talking with anyone about Jesus is that you—by virtue of your own Christian faith—have been *called* to do it. Having received Jesus and been brought into friendship with him, you, like Paul on the road to Damascus, have become enlisted in a great effort to bring the whole world to him so that the whole world can be saved from sin and death.

The second thing to know is that, though it might take you a while to get going, sharing Jesus is generally a pleasant activity, one you can do with friends, and one that can bring unexpected rewards.

The third thing to know is that you are not going to fail. We can promise you that. You are *guaranteed not to fail.*

Are we telling you that every time you talk to someone about Jesus, that person will come to Jesus?

No.

Are we saying that *most* of the time the person will come to Jesus?

Nope.

So, we're saying that sometime, at least one time, *some* person will come to Jesus?

Not even that.

We don't know what will happen once you start talking to others about Jesus. What we are telling you is that you are called to talk to others about Jesus, and all you have to do to be successful in answering this call is *to talk to others about Jesus*. What happens after that isn't for you—or us, or anyone else—to worry about. If you do what you have been called to do, that is success. Anything that follows from your efforts is up to God.

Now, in our experience, you will find that some of the people you talk with do come to Jesus. Some will return to Mass. Some will turn from atheism. Lots of great things are likely to happen. But none of that is for you, or us, or anyone who talks about Jesus, to worry about.

He is not asking us, nor has he ever asked us, to "convert" others, not even our family members. Whether people convert to the Faith or refuse the Faith is ultimately out of our hands. We are to carry the news, share the story, make sure that people have had a chance to hear it, and, if at all possible, to hear it in a personal and direct way.

Certainly, if they respond, there is much more we can do. We can help people to get their questions answered, to learn Scripture and Church Tradition, and many other things. What we cannot do is make anyone respond. Instead, we can *propose*.

Quite clearly one of the difficulties we will face as we propose Christ is that the fast-paced, media-saturated, and morally confused world we live in has, in many ways, hardened people against him. Vast numbers of people today believe that the age of Christianity has passed and the age of personal spiritualities has replaced it. Such people don't like Christians telling them that Christianity is unique, and that having faith in Jesus is the only way to the fullness of truth and light—to eternal life.

Also, many people today believe that Christian morals are outdated, even offensive.

There is real conflict in the world over the man Jesus. When people accuse us of offense when we proclaim Jesus as the only Lord, we cannot claim to have been misunderstood. We might not have been misunderstood at all. It is true that we believe many things that the world rejects and we reject many things that the world believes. For the Christian there is one Faith, and one Lord, Jesus. He is not a myth or a story. He is not just another wise man. He is the Savior and the Lord, the God become man who lived on earth, died, and rose from the dead.

This kind of absolute talk turns modern people off. Our era avoids these realities because it prefers less rigid religious ideas and less challenging moral requirements.

To talk about Jesus in such an atmosphere thus poses challenges. It makes the transmission of the gospel harder. But the very features of our society that create these challenges for the gospel also create an urgency that should encourage us to talk about Jesus.

Great suffering has accompanied the modern world's turn from Jesus. The world that hardens hearts against Jesus is also a wounded world, one in which the need for explicit talk of Jesus is all the more needed.

The idea that, if people could move beyond Christianity, society would be healthier, happier, less tormented by religious fixations, and freer to plot its own course was always mistaken. But in recent decades, as Christianity has faced actual collapse in many places, the consequences of the mistake are becoming clear.

 Don't be afraid to respond affirmatively to God's call. Your "yes" could echo in eternity!

De-Christianizing has not worked. People are not happier.

All around you, now, you see people who need healing but are unable to turn to the one who can heal because they have been convinced that any such turn to Jesus is a turn backward.

These people need guidance, but they can no longer hear the voice of the one who can bring them to joy, peace, and love. They have dismissed Jesus. They have not understood who he is.

In part, this is because what they *have* heard has been filtered through and distorted by hostile media. It is hard to exaggerate how much and how often Christianity has been made to look ridiculous or even sinister in movies, TV shows, books and newspapers, and online. And even where there is not intentional hostility to or gross ignorance about the Christian message, media consumption often devastates the life of faith. Popular entertainment appeals to people's lower appetites because to do so—to give people images of sex or wealth or revenge—is a well-trod path to riches. This constant stimulation of our base instincts has damaged countless souls, made them cold to divine things. To call people up higher, to ask them to give up selfishness, to challenge them to be truly self-giving in loving God and neighbor, is in contrast hard and unglamorous work.

The media try to submerge us in foolish and empty things. Christ calls us to come up out of them. He calls us to follow the narrow way, which is a more difficult path than the wide road that leads to destruction. This means that those who have encountered Christianity only through the distortion of modern media—those who have never known a Christian family, or been loved in a Christian manner, or been taught to reconcile faith and reason—tend to internalize, without really thinking about it, an idea that Christianity is a backward and unhappy philosophy.

Don't Hide the Cure

Of course, the fact that many modern people have not truly been introduced to Jesus and may, therefore, be personally inculpable for rejecting him, does not take away the consequences of lives lived apart from the Savior.

We have already mentioned the terrible suffering and confusion the world now bears because of the loss of Christ. And, sadly, we must add a word about the possibility of eternal suffering. Souls are in danger of being lost.

The mystery of damnation also prompts us to be bold in talking with people about Jesus. This was the motivation that drove century after century of Christian evangelizing, all the way back to the apostles themselves. Jesus is clear that eternal souls are at stake! In addition to the suffering all around us, the knowledge that souls can be lost gives us every incentive to talk about him. We know that Jesus can save souls, lives, families, and even whole nations.

And, finally, if compassion for the suffering in this world, and for the possibility of suffering in the next, were not motivation enough, we have the commands of Jesus himself and the constant exhortations of the Church to take up the work of sharing the Faith.

Matthew ends his Gospel with Jesus' command to "make disciples of all nations" (28:19). This ending has the dual effect of making it clear, in a final sense, what Jesus has spent three years preparing his disciples for and, also, making it clear to us, who have just finished reading the Gospel, what

 There are many kinds of love. There is no greater love than helping someone find salvation.

we are now supposed to do.

The apostle Paul, having seen the risen Jesus, said "an obligation is laid on me, and woe to me if I don't proclaim the gospel!" (1 Cor. 9:16).

This is true for everyone who has come to Christ. We must not receive the gospel of love and fail to love. Loving God, we must keep his commandment to go and make disciples; and, loving our neighbors, we must share with them the most precious gift: Jesus, who heals in this life and gives eternal life to all who accept him.

Imagine, for a moment, a doctor or scientist who discovered the cure for cancer but didn't share it with others. Would we call this person good? Would we admire this person? No, we would think this person did a great evil.

Well, we have something infinitely more valuable than the cure for cancer. We have the cure for spiritual death, and we must share it even if we're afraid or uncomfortable.

We must overcome our fear and discomfort. It can be done! And is being done every day. Even the most timid of Christians, with the help of God and of other Christians, are constantly taking up the challenge and finding that, though they weren't sure they could do it, they *can*. Many even find they're quite good at it.

The *Catechism of the Catholic Church* (CCC) forcefully affirms that we are all called to this work when it says,

> The disciple of Christ must not only keep the faith and live on it, but also profess it, confidently bear witness to it, and spread it. . . . Service of and witness to the faith are necessary for salvation (CCC 1816).

From Knowing to Sharing

But you almost certainly already know all of this, and accept it, because here you are reading this book. You *want* to tell others about what Jesus has done for you. You *want* others to hear the good news. Maybe in your family, maybe at work, maybe out in the wider world, you want to take up the great work given to the apostles, handed on by the saints, and still desperately needed today.

You already know that Jesus is good news. You know that everything about him is worth knowing and will make any person's life better. You know that to accept Jesus and to belong to him is to enter into the family of God, to possess eternal life, and to be freed from the consequences of sin and death. Those who come close to him will suffer heartaches and trials just like anyone, but they will be more joyful, less worried, less desperate, and more alive.

All Jesus asks of those of us who have already know him is to give other people a chance at this joy and life by sharing the truth with them. And whatever difficulties might come from sharing him, you will also find that the work comes with rewards. In fact, two recent popes, Paul VI and Francis, have used the words "delightful and comforting joy" to describe the act of evangelizing. Without denying the difficulties, we hope to help you share in this delightful and comforting joy.

Note: throughout this book, we will use phrases such as "talking to others about Jesus," "sharing the good news,"

The Church isn't a club: it's a lifeboat. We need to get people in!

and "evangelizing," interchangeably. It's all the same thing. In Jesus, God has come among us bringing healing, knowledge, hope, and salvation from sin and death. Whatever terms we use for it, what we mean is sharing this reality with others, passing on the news of something that happened in history and is still happening today.

Hard Work, Lasting Joy

The very first words Jesus spoke in the first Gospel written about him were, in fact, delightful and comforting: "The time is fulfilled, and the kingdom of God has come near; repent, and believe in the good news" (Mark 1:15).

Everywhere Jesus went proclaiming his new and exciting message, it was received with happiness.

It is also striking to read Matthew's account of the joy that broke out as Jesus began his ministry of healing and teaching. In chapter four of his Gospel, Matthew says that Jesus "went about all Galilee, teaching in their synagogues and preaching the gospel [good news] of the kingdom and healing every disease and every infirmity among the people. So his fame spread throughout all Syria, and they brought him all the sick, those afflicted with various diseases and pains, demoniacs, epileptics, and paralytics, and he healed them. And great crowds followed him from Galilee and the Decap'olis and Jerusalem and Judea and from beyond the Jordan" (Matt. 4:23–25).

 The world is dying for truth. If you have it, don't keep it to yourself.

The fourth chapter of Luke's Gospel gives a shorter account of the same moment but conveys the same sense of delight at the coming of Jesus. Luke tells us Jesus "returned in the power of the Spirit into Galilee, and a report concerning him went out through all the surrounding country. And he taught in their synagogues, being glorified by all" (Luke 4:14-15).

What the Gospel writers are clearly conveying to us is that we are not meant to take up our duty of talking about Jesus as if it were a punishment or a test. It isn't meant to be some grim task. With Jesus, everything is new. Hope has come into the world, and we have been given this important news to share with others.

Certainly, the joy of evangelizing isn't a mere feeling. Sometimes we will struggle and suffer as we try to share Jesus. The joy of the work comes not from constant emotional consolation but from knowing that our will is set on doing what God has called us to do—and knowing that he is with us and loves us as we do so.

To grasp how joy is not just nice feelings, consider a fire-fighter running into a burning house to save a family. He certainly won't feel just sweetness and light as he battles the heat and smoke! Likely he will experience feelings of dread and danger. But he knows what he is doing is meaning-ful. It fulfills an important purpose. And it helps others. This knowledge, this sense of meaning, gives the firefighter strength and life that he could not have if he had not pushed through his negative feelings to do what is good and right.

This natural joy is a good analogy for the supernatural joy that is part of evangelizing discipleship. Accompanying Jesus in his work, and extending his work to others, means we share life more deeply with him. This real sharing of life is more powerful than any hardships that accompany it.

Some who are drawn to the work of sharing Jesus can,

frankly, get too wrapped up in their own feelings. If they don't feel joyful or happy to share the gospel, they think something is wrong. If they don't feel a sense of being compelled to share, they think they're not called.

This is a mistake. If we wait for our feelings to be just right, or if we wait until we sense some inner compulsion, we will probably never speak up. For most people, evangelization just doesn't come naturally. It is difficult to start conversations with random people, especially if you're shy. To do it, we need to push through whatever feelings are holding us back.

Having said this, it must be said that, for many people, having pushed through their reluctance and hardships, there is a palpable emotional reward. Our worst fears rarely materialize, and often—especially if we master a conversational style of evangelizing—we find we truly enjoy the conversations we have. Getting to that point is often just a matter of overcoming a few obstacles.

No Special Gift Required

Because you are reading this book, you are probably already past the first obstacle, the one most Christians face: they just never get the message that they are called to do it. They may never have been told about the universal call to evangelization. Or, if they have heard of this call, they may never have been seriously invited to consider how this call from Jesus applies personally to them.

Today, this situation is changing. Catholics are hearing more about the call to evangelization than we have in a long time. But there is still work to do to get this message out.

The next obstacle to evangelizing is that many Christians think they're either not equipped for this work or are not holy enough. They may feel that evangelization isn't their "charism" or isn't a fit for their personality. They might even think they're not educated enough.

But is it true that we might not be equipped enough to evangelize? Is it true that *you* are not equipped?

God gives different charisms to each one of us for the building up of the Church. Some people have a charism for hospitality, others for leadership or administration. Still others have charisms such as teaching, healing, intercessory prayer, evangelization, and so on. St. Peter himself tells us,

> As each has received a gift, employ it for one another, as good stewards of God's varied grace: whoever speaks, as one who utters oracles of God; whoever renders service, as one who renders it by the strength which God supplies; in order that in everything God may be glorified through Jesus Christ (1 Pet. 4:10-11).

But consider this: what if I don't have the charism of, say, hospitality? Does that mean I don't have to be hospitable?

Of course not. We are not excused from our Christian obligations just because we lack special gifts that help us carry them out. If we don't have an extraordinary gift for hospitality, we simply live out that virtue in an ordinary way, doing the best we can. If we don't have a charism for healing, we still try to help the sick and pray for them in ordinary ways. If we don't have a charism for leadership, we still lead when the ordinary circumstances of life call for it.

 Don't worry about saying everything perfectly all the time. Just say it with love, right now.

This is also true with evangelization. Without question, some people have a special charism for it, but it remains an ordinary duty of *every* Christian life. Just as with hospitality or care for the sick, every Christians is called to this work, even those who are not uniquely gifted.

No special feeling or gift is needed to do what all the baptized have been commanded to do. The call to evangelize even applies to shy people and introverts. It even applies to people who are nervous or uncomfortable with conversation. What each one of us needs is to find the *particular ways* we are called to evangelize. What is my role in this shared vocation of the whole Church?

Certainly, extroverts may find evangelization easier to initiate than introverts will, but introverts still need to evangelize. Some of the best evangelists, in fact, are introverts, who often develop skills for communicating that might reach a particular person where an extrovert might push that person away. Some introverts are extraordinary public speakers or have other unique gifts. Thus, although our personality might direct the ways we evangelize, it cannot be an excuse for failing to evangelize.

So, what if we just don't feel we have the required knowledge? What if our grasp of the Bible or Church teaching feels too thin? The truth is, it is extremely rare to find people who know the Bible as well as they could or should. And even among these rare people, who always has the right answer to every question about the Faith? Nobody.

Without question, study of the Bible and *Catechism*, the saints, and other helpful materials is important. Study can improve our skills. But we don't need a comprehensive knowledge before we start sharing the gospel.

If we are believers, if we know Jesus Christ, we already have the best and most important formation. To be a witness of the gospel, we just need to have been changed for the better by the gospel. As you will see in the pages that follow, often the very best tools for sharing the Faith are your own, personal reasons for accepting Jesus and the Church. Can you talk about these? Then you already have something important to share.

But surely *holiness* is necessary for evangelization, right? So, what if we are still working on our own sins and still struggling in the walk of faith?

We will get into the relationship between personal holiness and evangelization as we go along because, in fact, holiness is very important to evangelization. But for the moment it is enough to stress that we are not enabled to evangelize by our own power. If we are baptized and living the sacramental life, we are filled with the graces and powers that flow from it. When we talk with others about Jesus, these sacramental powers are far more important than any piety or sanctity we possess. In fact, awareness of our own weakness and dependence on God is healthy.

The most important holiness belongs to Jesus. It is more important than we can imagine. By the mere fact that we are disciples of Jesus Christ, sharing life with him because of our baptism, we can carry him to others even when we, ourselves, are imperfect vessels.

Though we must strive for holiness, we must also evangelize even when we are still a work in progress, far short of perfection. After all, if the apostles had waited until they were perfect before starting to evangelize, the gospel would never have left the little region of Judea!

Called Beyond Our Comfort

Although it is normal to experience resistance to evangelizing, most of our objections are rooted in misconceptions about what kind of person is suited to share Jesus. We mislead ourselves into thinking we are just not the kind of person who can do it.

The truth is, this notion is rooted in fear. We're not inadequate, just scared: scared of pushing people away, scared of losing friends, or scared of what people might think of us.

Evangelization can be scary. But do we want a Christianity that demands nothing of us? Is that what we were expecting? No, we just need to push through fear—because this work is so important.

The apostles were afraid of proclaiming the gospel, too; finally at Pentecost they received the Holy Spirit, who gave them boldness. But even after Pentecost, they needed to pray for more zeal and boldness for the proclamation of the gospel (Acts 4). To learn to rely on God and push through fear is part of gaining maturity in evangelization.

One of the ways we can learn to overcome fear and grow in this maturity is to be *strategic* when we evangelize. No one is saying that, because we're called to share the Faith, we should go around the workplace and just start randomly declaring the gospel message to our coworkers indiscriminately! We need to be more subtle than that.

We need to be as wise as serpents (Matt. 10:16). Serpents pay attention; they watch and wait for their moment.

 Jesus didn't tell us to stay where we are and be comfortable—he told us to go out and get to work.

As the *Catechism* puts it, we need to be "on the lookout" (905) for opportunities to evangelize. In other words, we are not called to preach the gospel audibly at every moment, but we do need to make the furthering of the gospel a priority in our lives. And we need to learn how to create or foster opportunities in small ways. Maybe we start by giving Miraculous Medals or holy cards to our acquaintances. Or maybe we offer to pray with people who seem to need it. There are lots of little things we can do to get started.

Public speakers often talk about the fear that comes just before they take the stage, only to evaporate as soon as they start talking. They learn that the fear is no more than a momentary jolt that soon passes. If they just let it be and don't pay too much attention to it, the fear has no power. It's just a thing the mind and body do at moments of anticipation. It subsides once they take the stage.

Those who are new to public speaking can begin to panic in such moments, imagining all the things that could go wrong, wondering why they ever let themselves agree to do this. They might even let fear cause them to avoid public speaking—and thus never find out what every experienced public speaker eventually learns: it's not as bad as the mind makes it, and it can even be enjoyable.

Starting small, practicing, working with others who are experienced at evangelization, and avoiding unrealistic expectations of immediate results: all of these will help. And remember, if fear and worry are natural responses, they will ultimately be no match for the supernatural help that God gives those who desire to share him.

How to Use This Book

This book is divided into three parts:

First, we will present a refresher on the age-old gospel message as presented by Jesus, the disciples, and all the great evangelists throughout the ages of the Church. One of the troubles the Church has encountered in its evangelizing efforts in recent decades is a failure among us, the Christian people, to grasp the full gospel message. Even among people who have received all the family support and instruction we normally associate with a thorough formation in the Faith, this failure has sometimes led to an inability to present the gospel in all its life-changing power. If we lack clarity about just what the real gospel message is—its full power—then even the best evangelization techniques will be drained of their effectiveness.

The second part is the longest section of the book, and it presents tips, techniques, and strategies for conversing with others about Jesus. These are meant to be practical helps, and we hope they will also build up your confidence to talk about Jesus. You can do it. You really can. Even if you don't see yourself as one who possesses the gifts or temperament of an evangelist, you have been called to it, and you can easily be equipped. Remember, God doesn't call the equipped, he equips the called.

Each person who knows Jesus has a part to play in sharing him. But none of us has been magically gifted to do this work alone. Here we will draw on what others have learned, becoming part of a community of disciples able to help us as we go.

The final section is not about techniques as much as it is about your own ever-deepening conversion to and communion with Jesus. Knowing him, being healed by him, following him closely: these are the most important things for anyone who wants to talk about Jesus. What brought you to the desire to share Jesus with others? That story—the story of what Jesus has done for you—is important. It is worth remembering and sharing. Even when it remains unspoken, it will play a vital part in any effort you make to share Jesus with others. And it is an ongoing story. The vine of faith either grows or dies. Part three is about helping it grow.

In between chapters, there will be short counterpoints for your reflection. Some of them are scriptural lessons or meditations; others, where applicable, are drawn from the stories of ordinary people who took up the call to evangelize. All of these are meant to help to color and frame our themes.

The Spirit Is Moving Within You

"The love of God is everlasting," Pope Benedict XVI wrote in a 2011 message for World Day of Prayer for Vocations. "Yet the appealing beauty of this divine love, which precedes and accompanies us, needs to be proclaimed ever anew, especially to younger generations."

Whatever our particular vocations, each of us shares in this universal call to make the person of Jesus known to the whole world. It is in Jesus that the "appealing beauty" of divine love is truly and fully revealed. Year by year the need for him in every part of the world seems to become more urgent.

That urgency need not produce anxiety in us, however, because he has given us the tools. If we let him, he will empower us. At this very moment, the Holy Spirit is moving powerfully in the Church, enlightening it, providing it with new movements, and filling it with new enthusiasm. We should have every confidence, then, that the same Spirit who is moving in the world is moving in us and also moving in those to whom we hope to speak.

Most especially at this urgent moment, you have every reason to be confident that if the love of God has made a home in your heart, and if you will be docile to what the Church teaches, you can talk to anyone about Jesus.

PART ONE

Know the Message

1
Know the Full and Balanced Gospel

Do you know the gospel?

If you had to sum up the gospel in just a few words, could you?

Could you get in an elevator with someone and communicate the gist of the good news of Jesus Christ in the time it took to reach your floor?

The pace of modern life is intense, and this pace brings with it a ruthless pressure to communicate quickly, to *get to the point*. People are rushed. The world is rushed. We are anxious not to abuse other people's time. And we know that people today rapidly filter out information they don't feel they need. People dismiss ideas that they find suspect almost instantly because they don't think they have time to deliberate over them.

Many people who want to bring others to Jesus respond to this high-pressure reality by trying to reduce the gospel to its absolute minimum. Probably the best-known example

 One simple word about Jesus could change someone's eternity. You will never know which unless you say it.

of this is the sign held up at sporting events displaying just a word and some numbers: "John 3:16." Or a line drawing of a fish on a car bumper.

These brief communications are great. They are important. They encourage other Christians, and they might well lead to conversations with non-Christians. But they are only *reminders* of the gospel. They point to it rather than present it.

More is needed. Evangelization requires an explicit presentation of the gospel, leading, if all goes as one hopes, to an invitation to accept the Lord.

If we truly want others to come to Jesus, we must learn to share the whole gospel with all its essential parts. Having done so, we can then openly and honestly invite others to accept what Jesus offers in his Church. Certainly, the gospel can be expressed in a succinct and inviting way, but we must guard against the temptation to make our presentation so short, or—what is worse—so tame, that it loses crucial parts of its content.

Here, it is vital to have faith in the working of the Holy Spirit, who opens hearts and enlightens minds. It is the job of the Spirit to make converts. Our job is much, much simpler: to make sure that others are told and invited. Without question, we should try to be as effective as we can, employing the very best stylistic and conversational skills. And, indeed, there will be times when we can only present a fraction of the gospel either because of time constraints or because we intuit that the other person is only ready for part of the message. But in every case, we must be faithful to the fullness of the message.

Gradual, But Never Misleading

Even when we present the gospel in stages, we must do so in a way that does not mislead other people about the full content. A full and honest presentation is what we are called to give, whether in stages or in one complete presentation.

Consider this admittedly dramatic but not uncommon example: you are speaking with someone who

1) is an atheist,

2) is a habitual drug abuser, and

3) believes that Catholics worship a cracker.

Should you try to tackle all this at once? Should you defend the Eucharist? Focus on the drug abuse? Just start with the reality of God and leave it at that?

Clearly, the correct approach depends on the situation, your relationship to the person, the amount of time you have, and a host of other considerations.

What a faithful evangelist cannot do, however—even if the evangelist decides to take the gradual approach—is misrepresent the gospel. A true evangelist will never violate or undermine the message by, for example, making light of the importance of Eucharist or saying untrue things such as, "God doesn't really care about drug abuse." Even if only a part of the gospel is presented, the whole of the gospel must be respected. Otherwise, we will end up presenting a false gospel.

 By all means, meet people where they are. But don't be afraid to lead them where they need to go.

Working incrementally toward the fullness of the gospel can make sense. But being sneaky or misleading, even if it's to try to ease a person's acceptance of the truth, is wrong both on practical grounds (it is unlikely to work) and on moral grounds (it is a betrayal of Jesus).

What someone receives when he receives the gospel in its fullness is the person of Jesus Christ. If we present the gospel in a way that we think might make the listener more comfortable because it hides the fullness of who Jesus is and what Jesus has done, then what are we presenting? Are we truly evangelizing?

He is the way, the truth, and the life. He is the one who feeds us and heals us in the sacraments. To be introduced to the gospel is to be introduced to this one man, who is God enfleshed.

Four Parts, One Gospel

This brings us back to the question we began with: if you had to sum up the gospel in just a few words, could you? If you had to convey it succinctly without robbing it of any of its power, what would you say?

For too many people, the answer is something like this: "God loves you."

To be certain, we're not against the idea that God loves you. God does love you. And sometimes the words "God loves you" are exactly what a person needs to hear. But sometimes they are not.

The fact is, the truth that God loves you is the most important truth in the world, but it is not the gospel in its fullness.

For one thing, *love* is a problematic idea in today's world. The modern secular person and the Christian person are likely to mean very different things when they use the word. For the modern person, raised on countless hours of modern media, "love" is not thought of as an act but as a feeling. When the feeling is missing, they think there is no love. This can easily lead to a misunderstanding of divine love—which is the will of God to share with each person everything that God is and has.

But when Christians talk about love, we are talking about an *act*. To love another person is to *will his good*. If a woman shows up behind you in the grocery line in a terrible hurry and asks to go ahead of you, and you let her because it will do her good, that is love. It is a very small act, but it has a very big meaning—you have actively willed for another person to have a good that she didn't earn or, in strict justice, deserve. It doesn't matter how you *felt* about her, or even if you felt anything at all. Your active will for that other person's good is what mattered.

Thus, when a Christian speaks of God's love, we don't mean that God has feelings of tenderness and compassion for us. Nor, when Jesus tells us to love our neighbor, do we think he is telling us to have tender and compassionate feelings for our neighbor.

Such feelings are good. It is nice to have them. But they are not love.

When Christians say "love," we mean the act of the will that the other receive what is good.

We truly love another person when we live as if the good of that person is also our own good. Sometimes this will

When you speak the truths of the gospel, all heaven leans in to listen.

37

involve feelings of tenderness and compassion, sometimes it won't. What matters is the act of the will.

To actively desire that another should live and flourish, to actively desire that another should grow toward perfection (including moral perfection), to actively desire that another should possess all that God desires for them—this is to love.

God's will is for you to live and flourish, for you to come to perfection, and for you to possess all he has to give you. This can, in fact, be a very challenging love to accept. We might feel satisfied with lower goods—money, pleasure, power—where he wants us to have higher goods—virtue, freedom from sin, eternal life.

We often resist God when he tries to give us the higher goods because we want the lower ones. We can easily end up in conflict with God, turning away so that we can do as we wish.

To have the goods he intends for us, most especially eternal life shared in communion with him and with all the angels and saints, we must accept his help given in Jesus. This help rescues us from corruption and makes us his own children. We must repent, change, and live the new life he offers.

So, when a Christian sums up the gospel as, "God loves you," what do secular people hear? Is it just that God has warm feelings for them? If so, might this not simply reinforce the secular idea that God does not expect much of them?

Another way modern people think about love is even more off the mark: that love is simply being kind and refusing to criticize or condemn. This way of thinking about love is one of the consequences of the sexual revolution, in which people are supposed to be free to express themselves sexually without restrictions. This is an irresponsible and self-centered view of love that imagines happiness as a matter of feeling pleasure or "getting my way," free from judgments.

If we truly want to help people to grasp the importance of Jesus and the life of faith, we must put the good news into context. The full story must be told so that people can locate their own place in it, and that means sharing some bad news.

The Four-Part Gospel

Yep. There is bad news; and, if we really love others, we have an obligation not to hide it.

Rather than just one part of the good news—"God loves you"—modern people need to hear a *four*-part gospel.

In addition to the good news about God's love, for instance, they need to hear about *sin* (even if we don't use that word). Only when we have admitted that we have turned away from God and rejected his friendship can we understand that the fullness of the gospel is a rescue story, with Jesus as the one who rescues us.

Thus, our "elevator" presentation must be a bit more than a single sentence. It will need to be not just a simple statement but a *story:* about the loss of God and his movement to rescue us. And it is possible to share this before we reach our floor! The four-part story looks like this:

Part One: *Good News*—God exists, he loves you, he has a plan for your life. God *is* love. He created us and gave us this world because he loves us.

Part Two: *Bad News*—We are sinners and have broken that relationship. We have all fallen short of his glory by sinning. By our own choices, we have brought cruelty and suffering into the world, and we have lost the grace of friendship with God.

Part Three: *Good News*—God has not left us in this condition but has come in the flesh to rescue us. Jesus came to open the path to heaven, giving himself on the cross to ransom us from sin and death. And all who accept him and keep his commandments will find healing and will live with him forever in peace.

Part Four: *Our Response*—We need to respond by having faith in him, repenting of our sins, accepting baptism, and living the Church's life of faith.

This is the gospel as the apostles taught it. This mix of good and bad news and the call for a response was present from the very day of Pentecost, when the Holy Spirit first filled the Church with the power to preach.

On that day, Peter drew upon the whole story of salvation familiar to his Jewish audience to tell them good news. But he also included the bad news that they, just weeks before, had personally rejected the Lord when he was with them in the flesh. "Let the entire house of Israel know with certainty that God has made him both Lord and Messiah, this Jesus whom you crucified" (Acts 2:36).

With these words, Peter laid out the full consequences of sin. This brought forth a powerful reaction from the crowd:

> Now when they heard this, they were cut to the heart and said to Peter and to the other apostles, "Brothers, what should we do?" Peter said to them, "Repent, and be baptized every one of you in the name of Jesus Christ so that your sins may be forgiven; and you will receive the gift of the Holy Spirit. For the promise is for you,

for your children, and for all who are far away, everyone whom the Lord our God calls to him." And he testified with many other arguments and exhorted them, saying, "Save yourselves from this corrupt generation." So those who welcomed his message were baptized, and that day about three thousand persons were added. They devoted themselves to the apostles' teaching and fellowship, to the breaking of bread and the prayers (Acts 2:37-42).

Here Luke, the author of the Acts of the Apostles, demonstrates the full power of the gospel when it is presented and received honestly!

Peter didn't try to sugarcoat the evil of the crucifixion but included this sinful action as part of his message. Those who accepted what Peter said, and responded by taking action, received every gift that Jesus has given. They were able to receive the fullness of the apostolic teaching and all the sacramental gifts because they became convinced that they needed them.

Without question, in this instance Peter tailored his presentation of the gospel to his audience. He knew they were a Jewish audience that was familiar with Scripture, so he quoted Scripture to them, situating Jesus within the familiar Jewish history of prophets and kings to make his story understandable. Later, when presenting the gospel to gentiles, Peter would use other methods. But whatever rhetorical method he uses, the content of the gospel and its power to overcome sin and death are the same: the fatherly love of

 There is only one sure way that the world stays lost—we stay silent.

God, the awful reality of sin, the salvation offered by Jesus, and the response of faith, hope, and love.

In presenting both the good and bad news of the story of Jesus, Peter pierces the hearts of his listeners. This allows them to respond by entering unreservedly into the new life offered in the Church.

We want people to understand that God loves them, but we also want them to know the value of this love in their lives. This value cannot be understood unless the person knows the full story. Jesus cannot be understood, and very likely won't be truly accepted, if he is presented outside of this context.

At heart, the Catholic evangelist wants everyone to have what Peter and the apostles gave to the people of Jerusalem after Pentecost: repentance and baptism; forgiveness of sins and the reception of the Holy Spirit; salvation from corruption; teaching, fellowship, the eucharistic bread, and a life of prayer.

It was only because Peter was able to share the full truth of the gospel and show the crowd how to respond to that truth that the 3,000 Pentecost converts came all the way into the newly born Church, accepting its teachings and receiving its sacraments.

No Gospel Without Repentance

The Church's teaching on the bad news of sin and the call to repent are not distractions from the gospel—they are *essential* to the gospel. God loves us as we are; and he loves us *so* much that he won't *leave* us as we are.

For that reason, before we get into techniques for sharing the gospel, we must be clear and confident that the gospel we will set out to share is the same gospel Jesus and his apostles taught.

We want people to know that God loves them and created them for love. But we also want people to know that, by failing to love and obey God, we can, and do, turn our backs on his love, walk away from his friendship, and cut ourselves off from him.

Finally, we want people to *take action,* because the story doesn't end with the bad news. Jesus has come to repair all that is broken, and he has given us the means, if we respond to him, to accept his help and receive his gifts, to be restored to God.

The gospel, when accepted in its full power, opens a person to receive gifts. The highest of these gifts is the sharing of life with the Blessed Trinity. Near the end of his life, Jesus refers to this gift:

> I will ask the Father, and he will give you another Advocate, to be with you forever. This is the Spirit of truth, whom the world cannot receive, because it neither sees him nor knows him. You know him, because he abides with you, and he will be in you. I won't leave you orphaned . . . because I live, you also will live. On that day you will know that I am in my Father, and you in me, and I in you . . . Those who love me will keep my word, and my Father will love them, and we will come to them and make our home with them (John 14:15-23).

Our sincere hope is that, as you read through what follows, you will gain confidence in the power of the full gospel message and in your ability to share this gospel in a way that unleashes its power in the lives of others.

Given all the evil in the world, it can get pretty hard to argue that people are essentially good. In fact, many modern people would argue that we are not good. Misunderstanding science, some assume that life is an accident. Hurt and lost in a broken world, many feel worthless.

But, as Jesus says about divorce, so we can say about all the evil in our lives: "From the beginning it was not so" (Matt. 19:8).

Scripture makes it clear that we are, in fact, not evil or accidents but were specially created and created good. Psalm 139 calls us "wonderfully made" (139) and the very first chapter of the Bible tells us, "God created man in his own image, in the image of God he created him; male and female he created them. And God blessed them" (Gen. 1:27-28). For those who feel far from God, and who think of themselves not as good but as worthless or accidental, we must remind them of the first part of the gospel message: God made you and he loves you with a perfect, fatherly love.

2

Craft Your
Personal Message

In sharing Jesus with others, we are far more likely to succeed if we first take the time to craft our own message. Later, we will have more to say about prayer and the sacraments in the life of the person who wants to talk with others about Jesus. But, here, at the beginning, we need to be clear that—although we are always open to the possibility that we will be aided in our evangelizing by miracles, surprising movements of the Spirit, or powerful mystical experiences—we should not expect such things to do our work for us. If God has called us to share news of his Son, we should *prepare:* just as we would for a job interview, a first date, or a work presentation.

The first essential step in preparation is to know fluently each element of the four-part gospel we discussed in the previous chapter:

God is the creator who loves us.

 **Stop waiting for the perfect moment.
Souls are perishing now, so now is the moment.**

We have all sinned and fallen short of the glory of God.

Jesus has come to open heaven to us and restore us to the family of God.

We must respond by doing what he has called us to do, accepting him and living the life of faith.

The second essential thing is that we *craft our own, personal message* for presenting the gospel, suiting it to a world full of people who are in many different spiritual conditions.

In 1975, on the tenth anniversary of the Second Vatican Council, Pope Paul VI released the letter *Evangelii Nuntiandi*, in which he asked Catholics to take up with renewed vigor the great work of bringing the gospel to all people. Even today, many decades after Vatican II's conclusion, people ask just what that council was for. Why did all the world's bishops gather to do something that, in the whole history of the Church, had only been done twenty times before? Pope Paul's answer was simple: "To make the Church of the twentieth century ever better fitted for proclaiming the gospel to the people of the twentieth century."

And if the whole Church needed and still needs to be better fitted for the task of sharing Jesus, then each of its members—each of us—must also be better fitted.

The pope ardently desired his fellow Catholics to get out and proclaim the gospel in the modern world, and he suggested many ways to marshal modern communications, charitable efforts, schools, and families to the task. But he stressed most insistently the need for *personal evangelization*.

"In the long run," he asked, "is there any other way of handing on the gospel than by transmitting to another person one's personal experience of faith? It must not happen that the pressing need to proclaim the good news to the multitudes should cause us to forget this form of proclamation whereby an individual's personal conscience is reached and touched by an entirely unique word that he receives from someone else."

In this chapter, ask yourself: What is the "entirely unique word" you might share with another person? Consider that what makes this communication unique is that it is shared between real people. It reflects your own experience, and it is shaped especially for the person you are speaking with. What in your life, your story, and your own relationship with God can you draw on to communicate Jesus to others? And how might you express that story so that it responds to the needs of the other person?

The Gospel Is Personal

The communication of the gospel isn't like the communication of an impersonal or abstract idea such as a scientific theory or a mathematical proof. The sharing of these kinds of knowledge does not require an entirely unique word. The gospel message, on the other hand, is the *news of an event*—in which we evangelists have become caught up and to which your hearer is invited.

We who have come to friendship with Jesus have been caught up into the dawning of God's kingdom in the world. Through our life in the Church we have become privileged citizens of this kingdom. Knowing Jesus and having been sent by him, we testify not just to ancient things we have read about in books, but to new things, things we have experienced, a life we are living right now.

 God didn't give you saving grace and truth just for your own sake. He saved you so you can help save others.

If each of us puts the effort into crafting our own message, we can communicate Jesus as we have come to know him to people in a whole variety of different situations. In fact, we can develop the skill of sharing Jesus in a manner that fits the person we are talking with, a person, like us, with unique experiences and unique perspectives.

Crafting Your Own Message

As with any creative endeavor, each person will approach the process of crafting a message differently, but we can suggest the following steps:

1) *Identify the objective for your specific crafted message.* Perhaps you will be talking to a relative who has stopped practicing the Faith. In this case, your objective might be to get the relative to come to Mass with you one weekend. Or maybe you want to talk with an atheist who you know from work. In this case your goal might be to find an opportunity to share just one reason why you believe in God.

2) *Know your hearer's background.* Even if your message is entirely about what Jesus has done in your life, your message will be different, for example, if you are going to talk to a Baptist neighbor who knows the Bible than if you are going to talk to an unchurched neighbor whose only experience of Christians is on televi-

Speak the name of Jesus with love and confidence. There's power in it.

sion. If you're going to be talking with that Baptist, take some time to learn what Baptists believe. If your hearer is unchurched, familiarize yourself with such people's common obstacles to religion.

3) *Make sure the tone and language of your message are appropriate for your audience.* It isn't just the content of the message that must be fitted to the person, but the manner of speaking. Sometimes a tone of compassion is demanded because you are dealing with a person who is lost or in pain. But, on some occasions, a more intellectually or morally challenging tone might be needed.

4) *Organize your message in a logical manner.* Usually this means have a beginning, a middle, and an end. This might sound like simplistic advice, but you would be surprised how easy it is to become undisciplined in your message if you're not intentional about its structure!

5) *Incorporate personal testimony into your message, using examples, anecdotes, and analogies where appropriate.* If coming to Jesus meant you were able to overcome an addiction, or allowed you to forgive a cruel hurt, mentioning this might well be important, even if you don't go into great detail. Simple analogies can help support such details: "I was stumbling around as if in the dark and meeting him was like turning on a light."

6) *Make sure your plan includes practical and logistical details.* Could you invite the Baptist neighbor over for dessert some night? Are there times when you run into this same neighbor at the coffee shop? Do you have a shared interest or activity that you know will provide an opportune setting for evangelization? Do a

person's life circumstances provide specific openings or, conversely, recommend you avoid certain topics?

7) *Anticipate questions or objections that might come up.* At some point, that Baptist is probably going to say something like, "I don't need a priest to forgive my sins. I can go directly to God." Maybe you want to look up some common Catholic replies to this objection before your chat. On the other hand, many people will ask entirely innocent questions: "What is a sacrament?" or "Does it really matter what church I go to?"

8) *Revise, refine, practice, and get feedback from people you trust!* As you would with anything you want to get good at, work on your presentation by simplifying your message and taking out jargon or "churchy" sounding phrases. Strive for brevity and clarity. The Church offers many opportunities for help with this. We have already mentioned St. Paul Street Evangelization, and many parishes have evangelization teams that can be helpful. Campus ministry and Newman Centers can help. Religious orders have affiliate programs. And apostolates such as Catholic Answers can give you both ideas and support.

Believers, Not Yet Followers

As you craft your personal evangelization strategies, pay special attention to the message you craft for those who are nominally Christian but lukewarm or non-observant. In the West, in fact, most of the people you encounter will fall into this group! So, polishing your message for them is essential. If you genuinely want to help people to come into the full life of faith, you must take seriously the reality that we live in a world of fading faith. We are surrounded by millions of "baptized pagans"—lukewarm, poorly instructed, secularized Christians. This presents a vast field, ripe for evangelization.

Talking about Jesus with most people in the modern West, then, is usually not a matter of introducing them to something they have never heard of *at all*. Rather, today's evangelization is usually an attempt to get a person to re-evaluate something he has already heard or partly heard. He might know, or think he knows, the basics of Christianity, but has dismissed or abandoned it. Perhaps with prejudice—thinking of Jesus as a myth and religion as a harmful "opiate of the masses"—or perhaps simply ignoring it, as he seemingly enjoys his comfortable, secular, materialistic life. Whatever the case may be, such people are not wholly ignorant of the gospel.

Many of these are people we could call "believers who are not yet followers." They might not only be aware of the gospel; they also might believe or assent to much of what Christianity teaches. Yet they don't live it. They haven't fully committed themselves to God, and Christianity doesn't make any meaningful difference in the way they live.

Evangelizing such people is in some ways easier than evangelizing people who have never heard of Jesus. A person who has been baptized or received other sacraments has already received effects in the soul that have the power to assist faith. And those who have been even somewhat formed in Christianity have, in ways big and small, likely internalized at least parts of the gospel. The evangelist isn't starting

Heaven rejoices over the return of even one soul. You could help start that party.

from zero but has the easier task of bringing the power of the sacraments and any accompanying Christian formation back to life.

In other ways, however, evangelizing such people presents added challenges. One of the hardest things for any of us to fight is our *own habits*, and the person who has developed the habit of being a lukewarm Christian won't easily let it go. These habits were formed for a reason. Maybe the person never found Christianity all that convincing. Maybe he came to believe that God was not really concerned with his day-to-day life. Maybe he has cherished vices he doesn't want to give up. Maybe the person was hurt by other Christians, including parents or pastors, and prefers to keep the Church at arm's length.

We must craft our messages to such people in ways that account for these obstacles. This will help us to turn over the soil and plant seeds, knowing in faith that whatever obstacles might be keeping a person away from adhering to the gospel, God's grace can overcome them.

Principles of a Personal Message

When you say the name of Jesus out loud, you imitate and commune with the very first evangelists.

In crafting the story you want to tell, bear in mind that it's not an abstract presentation of some ideology. It is *personal*. It is about Jesus, and it is coming from you and is rooted in your own lived experience. Working from the basic, four-part message of the gospel, keep you message rooted in what Christ has done for *you*.

Maybe less, "Jesus came so that humanity can be healed," and more, "When I was stuck in anger and resentment, Jesus healed me."

Or, maybe, instead of "By transubstantiation the bread becomes the body of Christ," something more like, "I have found that sitting with Jesus in the Eucharist has brought me close to God in ways I could not have imagined."

What makes for a good personal message? There are some principles to observe. A good personal message:

1) *Sticks close to your own story.* Don't try to create a hundred different messages to suit every possible circumstance. (You are not likely to remember more than a few, anyway.) Your message can be adapted to your audience, but each one should stay true to your core experience.

2) *Is brief.* This is more important than many people realize, and a vital reason to craft your messages carefully. Catechism lessons are for later. Nobody wants to sit through a lecture; people are much more likely to listen to a short story.

3) *Doesn't come across as scripted.* Crafting your message isn't the same as memorizing a script, like a telemarketer. Work to become comfortable enough with your message that you can adapt on the fly depending on the direction that each conversation takes. The goal is to master your message so that you can have natural-sounding human conversations that include the points you want to communicate.

4) *Isn't bossy or critical.* You are *testifying,* not judging or giving orders. Good personal testimony isn't argumentative and does not make others feel argumentative. This is what makes it easier for others to hear and consider.

5) *Ends with an invitation.* We will talk more about this later, but it is worth mentioning here. The gospel calls for a response. A personal presentation of the gospel invites others to experience the peace and joy that it has brought to you.

Remember, too, that part of making a good testimony is knowing when to stop! Not every conversation you have about Jesus is going to include all the elements on your list. Sometimes telling a person that God loves him really is all you can do in the moment. Sometimes it's enough for now to assure the person you're praying for him. Silence that promotes reflection can be as useful as words. So, never get locked into a pressure mindset that says, "I have to say all these things, and say them *right now*."

For example, imagine talking with a coworker who just shared that he's going through a difficult period. When you start to explain how your faith helped you through a similar time, his eyes begin to well up. You pause and say, "Just know that God loves you, and I'll be praying for you." Right there, in that quiet moment, your simple words probably accomplished more than a full testimony ever could.

Go ahead now and give some thought to crafting your messages. Think about how you'll customize them for total unbelievers and for the lukewarm. Make them personal. Keep them brief and clear. Then, revise, refine, and practice each of these messages—out loud, to friends and family—until you feel comfortable with them.

Now you have the basic equipment for talking about Jesus to anyone. From these core messages, you can craft more specific messages for the people you are called to evangelize in your own life, as their needs and your relationship may suggest. No, you don't *know everything* or have an answer to every question. But you don't have to! In fact, no one has all the answers. So, it is always acceptable, when faced with hard questions, just to say, "I don't know. I'd like to take some time to investigate that and get you a solid answer."

Consider this rather common scenario. You find yourself chatting with a coworker during lunch when the topic of faith unexpectedly comes up. The coworker, curious but skeptical, asks why you believe in Jesus when there are so many religions in the world. You feel a wave of panic—you don't have a theology degree, and you aren't sure how to respond. But instead of shutting down, you simply share the basics: how Jesus changed your life, brought you peace, and gave you hope. When the conversation turns to more complex questions you simply admit, "I don't know, but I'd love to find a good answer and get back to you." This isn't an evangelization failure—it is a seed planted, and one that you can water by coming back with some answers later.

The point to remember is not that you have to be the best sharer of your message, but that you have the *best message to share.* Even though you're going to make mistakes, it's worth sharing—and you have what it takes to do it.

Prepare to Evangelize

Another reason to work at crafting your message, to think through and plan what you want to say to others about Jesus, is that going through this process reinforces the fact that you are *going to evangelize.* Not preparing to evangelize, frankly,

So what if you're "ordinary"? God always uses ordinary people to do eternal work.

makes it easier to never do it. In real life, does a moment so perfect that we know on the spot *just* what to say ever present itself? Not in our experience. Instead, those who go through life intending to talk about Jesus. but not preparing for it, rarely, if ever, find themselves doing it.

On the other hand, if we go to the trouble of crafting our message, we become ready. And if we are ready, we are evangelists. Now talking with others about Jesus is not just a thing we hope to do, it is a thing we are going to do—we just don't know when.

To get a sense of the way preparation makes things easier, just imagine how you'll feel on the day a friend mentions over lunch that he's been feeling lost lately and then wonders aloud if there's more to life. Because you've spent time thinking about how to share your faith, you're able to gently say, "I've felt that way too—and for me, getting to know Jesus changed everything." That kind of natural flow of evangelization comes from being ready and having a simple message ready.

Adapting Your Message

While we're crafting our message, we can also be praying that God sends us people to deliver it to and that God will make the message effective. God does not leave us to evangelize on our own but is always with us.

For example, Sarah was an older woman who felt a deep calling to share her faith, but she always felt tongue-tied. Encouraged by a friend, she decided that instead of trying to force conversations, she would pray. She prayed not just for the courage to speak, but specifically that God would lead her to someone who needed to hear a message of hope. She began to start each day with this quiet, fervent prayer, repeating it as she went about her errands.

Not long after she began this process, as she was sitting in a coffee shop, a woman at the next table spilled her entire cup of latte. Sarah rushed over to help, but the woman, she noticed, looked utterly defeated. Sarah asked if she was alright and the woman confessed, "Everything just feels like it's falling apart today."

Normally, Sarah would have mumbled an awkward "I'm sorry to hear that" and retreated. But this time, a gentle confidence settled over her. She asked if the woman wanted to talk, and as the conversation unfolded, Sarah realized this was exactly what she had prayed for. She shared a simple, heartfelt message of God's unwavering presence, even amid chaos. Emily said, "I really needed to hear that today."

Sarah left the coffee shop with a feeling of lightness. God hadn't left her alone. He had prepared the ground and given her the words to share.

That God is with us is a very encouraging thought, because few conversations go exactly as we hope or expect! Yet we know that God is always at work.

An evangelist we know has a friend named Judy, a woman who was raised Catholic but no longer practices her faith. The two of them speak from time to time and have a friendly, easy rapport. Once, in a casual conversation, Judy mentioned that her family used to attend Easter Mass when she was a child. It was just a passing comment, but it said a lot.

This evangelist is well aware that it isn't his job to make Judy come back to Mass, but he does feel called to share

 You don't need to have all the right answers— just the right attitude.

reasons for her to return and to extend an invitation when the moment feels right. With that understanding, the evangelist is free to speak about faith without pressure—just honestly and naturally. He just wants to plant the seed and let God bring the growth.

He's begun thinking intentionally about how he might open a meaningful conversation. Often, he asks Judy what she did over the weekend, and he has made up his mind that if she returns the question, he will mention attending Mass. He might even share a moment from the homily or readings that could resonate with her experience.

As he prepares to speak about Jesus, he thinks of it as "re-evangelizing"—not as a lecture, but as a moment of rekindling. Judy is baptized and familiar with Christian culture but perhaps has never heard the gospel presented in a way that truly speaks to her life now.

So, the evangelist crafts analogies tailored just for Judy. She's in the IT field, so he might grasp a comparison between reading the Bible and running regular software updates—something essential for stability and security. Or he might describe confession as a monthly reboot or system refresh. Or, because Judy is also passionate about fitness, he might compare going to Mass to working out—a spiritual training session—and the homily as coaching for the soul.

Ultimately, it's about meeting Judy where she is and inviting her to see faith from a new angle. The evangelist's goal is simple: to encourage one woman to consider returning to Mass and re-engaging with her spiritual roots. Because the evangelist has taken time to reflect on his own reasons for staying connected to the faith, he feels he'll be ready to share those reasons when the moment presents itself.

Of course, Judy might shut down that conversation by changing the subject or rolling her eyes. Or she might show a genuine and enthusiastic interest. He can't control this. But he can adapt to it.

If her response is negative, he might decide in the moment to press on to see where the conversation goes. Or he might let the topic drop for now and maybe bring it up another time in some other way. There is no absolute right or wrong answer most of the time. We have to make prudential judgments and do the best we can.

On the other hand, if she shows signs of being open to a faith conversation, he can listen to what she has to say, build bridges of understanding, and try to answer her questions. If this happens, he might find himself in a position to ask, "Can I share with you one good reason *I* go to Mass?"

Frequently, the things we planned to say end up not being quite right for the moment. But if we know our general message well, we can adapt to situations as they present themselves in real time. Having your messages well developed will mean that specific conversations won't be derailed if they don't go as you planned, because you will be flexible, open to and ready for each evangelizing moment when it comes.

Being prepared in general, but able to go where the conversation takes you, also fosters the trust in God without which evangelization can't succeed. It also makes the whole experience more pleasant—for you and for the other person!

Being prepared doesn't mean being perfect. There will always be things we don't know, questions we can't answer, and situations we are not sure how to respond to. But if we live the Faith, we have a story to tell. What we carry, the gospel, is the most important message in the world.

Modern life is a strange mix of anguish and arrogance. While some live with a terrible sense of worthlessness, others are overconfident. Such people have lost the sense of sin and the understanding that they owe God obedience. They don't feel in themselves the need for a savior because they don't experience their own need for forgiveness.

How will such people accept Jesus? For those who don't concern themselves with God's will and don't heed the Lord's warnings about injustice and immorality, we must find ways to make them aware of the second part of the gospel message: each of us needs a savior. Each of us must repent and reform our lives because "all have sinned and fall short of the glory of God" (Rom. 3:23).

PART TWO

Share the Message

3

Adopt the Four-Step Method

If you were holding a priceless piece of pottery and wanted to hand it to someone else, you would be *very* careful in how you did it. Because of its great value, you would do your absolute best to help the other person receive it safely and fully intact.

So it is with the proclamation of the gospel. It is so precious that we want to pass it on to others with the utmost care, so they can fully receive it, too. As with a priceless vase, we can't control what others do with it once in their possession, but we can control how we go about getting it there.

In this chapter, then, we will lay out a four-step process with each step designed to help you pass on our precious faith safely and effectively. In brief, the four steps are *Listen, Befriend, Proclaim,* and *Invite.* This structure is aimed at being both practical for the evangelist and respectful of the person

 First of all, close your mouth. Evangelization begins with listening, not preaching.

being evangelized. Further, it is meant to imitate the example of Jesus and the saints in their manner of evangelizing.

You can expect this method to build your confidence and give you a sense of direction as you seek to share your evangelizing messages. After all, even if each of us develops a well-crafted message that shares Jesus as we have come to know him, it will be of little use if we are never quite sure how to start, sustain, or conclude a conversation about faith. That's where our four steps come in.

Note at the outset that the method we offer here is certainly not meant to limit your prayerful creativity in finding other ways to share Jesus with others. If you are thinking there is no one-size-fits-all approach to sharing Jesus, we agree with you! The mission field is huge, and new ideas and approaches are always needed. But the four steps are a great basis from which to start.

None of us alive can take credit for inventing these steps. We recognize that even the best evangelizers can benefit from the hard-won lessons of the many saints and ordinary Catholics who have blazed a trail for us. That said, in sharing this method we will be drawing in a particular way on the years of effort put in by the many Catholics who have worked with St. Paul Street Evangelization (SPSE). Their direct experience in the field of evangelization, and their time together working constantly to improve their techniques, produced the Listen, Befriend, Proclaim, and Invite formula as we present it here.

As the founder of SPSE, Steve has seen street evangelists use this method time and time again. In countless real-life settings, these evangelists refined and improved their approaches. As Steve led this work and reflected upon it, he developed the language and ideas expressed in this book to train evangelists. Because Catholic Answers is a media ministry dedicated to helping Catholics understand, explain, and defend the Faith, working with Steve to find the widest possible audience for these ideas seemed a natural fit. That's how Steve and Cy, who is the host of *Catholic Answers Live* and an author, came to embark on this work together.

Everyone involved in this project is convinced that it is time for the whole Catholic Church to renew its commitment to sharing the gospel. Billions of people are in desperate need of Jesus *right now*. The world needs the fullness of the Catholic faith. Our aim is to help you as you participate in this mission of the whole Church. If you master these steps, you will add useful tools to your gospel-sharing toolbelt, so to speak, and these tools that can be adapted and applied in a great variety of situations. And far from locking you in one way of doing things, applying these steps will free you up to be creative and flexible as you present the gospel.

Understanding Your Audience

We are all familiar with the stereotype of the street preacher who shouts at passersby about the wrath of God and the salvation of the cross. There is often a good deal of bravery in this sort of preaching. It takes guts to go out in public loudly proclaiming Jesus as Lord and Savior, and it must be admitted that such preaching has led some people to Jesus. But even if such preaching sometimes proves effective, it also alienates most of the people who hear it. What about the people who rush by trying to avoid any contact with the speaker? Is there some way we could reach *them* with the gospel?

What if we could see them in a coffee shop later and ask them, "Would you mind telling me why you just rushed past without listening to that message?"

What might they say? After all, the message is an important one—it involves their eternal destiny—so why not stop to consider it?

You would probably get a great variety of answers. Some would tell you they don't believe in God; others that the speaker made them nervous. Some would say they reject that kind of judgmental religion; others might reply they already know Jesus and already go to church.

It is this great variety of answers that most makes clear the disadvantage of the shouting-at-strangers method. The person who uses it never knows anything about the people he is preaching to. He is just announcing a general message into the air and hoping it will find a receptive ear.

But what if there were some magical means by which the street preacher could come to know what was in the minds and on the hearts of each person walking past? Wouldn't that knowledge change him? Wouldn't knowing what they desired, what they were worried about, what they hoped for, and what they feared, soften his heart toward them as fellow human beings and shape his message so that it responded to their needs?

Wouldn't it be a great advantage to him as a preacher to be able to choose his presentation of the Faith based on the circumstance and experiences of each soul that passed by?

Well, of course, there *is* a way to know what is in another person's mind and heart, and it isn't magic. We can know *when they tell us*. All we must do is listen. When we allow other people to tell us their stories, to raise their objections,

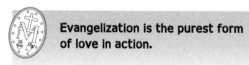

Evangelization is the purest form of love in action.

to ask for what they need, then we have a window into the mind and heart that we cannot get in any other way.

Won't this knowledge soften our hearts to them as fellow human beings causing us to shape our message so that it responds to their needs?

And what if we did more than just listen? What if we responded with compassion, found common ground, and did all the things that help build bonds of friendship between ourselves and the other person? What if we did this even when the other person says things we don't agree with or acts in ways that we don't approve of?

If we have listened to another person, and if we have tried to befriend that person, won't we be in a better position to proclaim the gospel? And—equally importantly—won't the other person be, at least a little, more disposed to receive our message respectfully?

After all, we don't just want to *talk at* people about Jesus. We want to have *conversations with them* that allow them to truly receive the gospel. What gives us the greatest chance to have such a conversation? What gives us the greatest chance of helping another person come closer to God? Indeed, how can each of us be a channel of grace so that the Holy Spirit might bring about the conversion of heart and mind that will allow another person to know the love of God given in Jesus?

These are the questions we hope to provide some answers to in the following chapters because instead of a one-size-fits-all message, Jesus, himself, has a personal message for each soul. Do we imagine his words would be the same to the person who has been hurt by Christians and the person who just wants to avoid moral living? Would he have the same message for the person who finds Christianity at odds with science and the person who has just been too busy to return to church, despite wanting to?

Does he have the same message for everyone he meets in the Gospels?

He does not. He meets people where they are, and we are meant to imitate him in that. This is the path to truly effective evangelization, leading to meaningful conversions and deeper encounters with God's love.

Walter, a naturally shy man, found confidence in the four steps of evangelization: Listening, Befriending, Proclaiming, and Inviting. He realized it wasn't about a rigid script, but an adaptable structure that allowed him to genuinely connect with people. He'd start by listening intently to their stories and building a friendship based on trust and mutual respect. Only then, when the timing felt right, would he gently begin proclaiming the message of Christ, eventually inviting them to explore faith more deeply.

This method wasn't about simply talking at people; it was about fostering genuine discussions that opened hearts and minds to God's boundless love, a process that made Walter feel surprisingly capable in sharing his faith.

4

Make Friends for Jesus

It is not at all an exaggeration to say that personal evangelization—speaking directly with others about Jesus—derives its unique power, before anything else, from the first two steps: *listening* and *making friends*.

Jesus described himself as the vine and his followers as branches. Pope St. John Paul II referred to this image as revealing the identity and dignity of the Christian, because in this image we see the Christian, as a branch as the one who bears the life of Christ out into the world. Through Christians, Christ the vine reaches particular people right where they are.

The great advantage the individual branches have is that we can get to know people. This is the super-power, so to speak, of the countless millions of branches who make up the Church.

When a branch of the Church (one of us) gets to know a particular person and becomes a friend to that person, that branch (you, for example) takes on a usefulness that no preacher in the pulpit or influencer on a screen can have, no matter how filled with talent and grace. The branch becomes useful because the branch makes direct contact with a person who otherwise would stay unconnected with the vine. Listening to and befriending others permits personal sharing on the level of the heart and the mind.

Especially in a world filled with advertising insincerity and consumer cynicism, this direct knowledge of and love for the one being evangelized has immeasurable value. The person has the opportunity to hear the gospel not as a remote ideology, but as a personal message for him.

If all an evangelist does is talk, talk, talk, the gospel message can be rendered powerless, because his hearers are not personally engaged. If anything, they are probably annoyed.

For this reason, and others that we will get to, listening and befriending must come first. These are the beginning steps in personal evangelization.

This, frankly, is why romantic relationships are often fertile ground for sharing the Faith. Certainly, there are instances in which one spouse comes into the Church as a condition of marriage or just to help create harmony in the home. But many other times, a spouse hears the gospel with openness *because* of the love shared in the home. The friendship shared by the husband and wife allows for the non-Christian or non-Catholic spouse to encounter the gospel with trust. The openness of heart that this trust engenders allows room where perhaps there was no room before for faith.

Whether we hope to talk about Jesus with our adult children who have left the Faith, with a friend who has never come to the Faith, or with a complete stranger on the street, our best efforts will always include these two steps.

Soften the Heart–and Open the Ears

Everyone wants to be heard, but especially in our era of loneliness and isolation, people often experience a profound ache for anyone they can talk to. Many are desperate, in fact, to encounter someone, anyone, who will listen.

Likewise, in our increasingly rude and selfish world, there is a great hunger for friendship, even to hear just a single friendly word. One of the greatest shocks some beginning evangelists encounter is the many people who are deeply touched when the evangelist listens attentively and builds bridges of friendship. Especially for new evangelists who assume they will face a great deal of resistance to the gospel, it can be a great source of joy to find how many people are delighted to talk, to share, and to engage in friendly conversation.

At the most basic level, Christian evangelization is about friendship because Christianity is about friendship. Jesus came to restore friendship between God and man, and, in doing this, to restore us all to peace and friendship with one another.

To accomplish his mission, Jesus gathered men and women to himself, he took years building up friendships with them, and then he sent his friends out to call others.

Just before he went to his death, Jesus said, "I have called you friends, because I have made known to you everything that I have heard from my Father" (John 15:15). Notice that friendship with God is connected, in this statement of Jesus, to *receiving knowledge*. Without the knowledge revealed by Jesus—particularly the knowledge of God's love and mercy—we are lost and cannot be restored to friendship with God. But once given the revelation of God in Jesus, his disciples were able to become his friends because they were able to repent of their sins and accept God's love and mercy.

This is what it means to share the gospel: to pass on the revelation of God in Jesus so that those who receive it can be restored to friendship with God and with one another. And

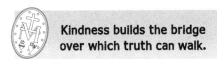

**Kindness builds the bridge
over which truth can walk.**

that is, at root, what the evangelist does—extend the invitation, first made by Jesus himself, to share in the life of divine friendship.

Unfortunately, today many people, including many Christians, have been infected with a media image of evangelization as something that judges others and imposes on their freedom. Is it any surprise that so many Christians avoid evangelizing when evangelizing has been given such a bad reputation?

Would you want to be friends with the kinds of Christians you see in most movies or on TV? If a character on TV or in a movie is shown wanting to talk about Jesus, that character is almost guaranteed to be weird, probably a hypocrite, and maybe even dangerous. This kind of media representation has, over time, created anxiety in many Christians. *We* don't want to be like that. We don't even want to be thought of that way, so we are careful not to be too open in how we talk about Jesus.

But real Christian people are not like the ones in movies. Most evangelists—Christians so alive in their faith that they want to go out and share Jesus with others—are normal, considerate people. They make and keep friends as easily as anyone else.

In fact, friendship is one of the great unsung joys of evangelization. Consider this real story of one Catholic street evangelist:

> *Once I was evangelizing at a fair, and we were passing out rosaries. We asked a man if he'd like a rosary, and he said, "No way. That's Catholic."*
>
> *I said, "Oh, you're not Catholic? Do you believe in God?"*
>
> *He said he was a Christian, and I asked him what his issue with Catholics was. He said, "Well, first of all, you Catholics don't read the Bible."*

What I wanted to say was something along the lines of, "We read the Bible! We hear the Bible at Mass, we're responsible for the canonization of the Bible. The only reason you have a Bible is because of the Catholic Church!"

But, instead, I responded, "You know, you're right."

Instantly, this put us on shared ground and opened the possibility for a friendly encounter.

So, I went on, "Catholics don't read the Bible enough. It's true. The Bible is the word of God, and we need to be reading it more often!"

And then I was rolling. I said, "You know what, I don't read the Bible enough either. I try to read the Bible every day, but I should be reading it more. It's the word of God! I bet most people in your church don't read the Bible enough either. Do they?"

He said, "You're right, they don't."

I asked, "Do you read the Bible enough?

He said, "Not as much as I should."

After a few minutes of conversation, I had my arm around his shoulder and we were both shaking our heads that nobody reads the Bible enough. He walked away from that table with the rosary, some pamphlets on the Bible, and a book by Scott Hahn.

That wouldn't have happened if I had gotten defensive. Instead, by the grace of God, I went a different direction, was able to find common ground, and ended up actually befriending him.

If we become good at listening charitably and building genuine bridges of friendship with others, we will find opportunities to talk openly and honestly about Jesus and his Church. And this is what we want. We want whatever friends we make to know that Jesus is our primary friend, and he can be theirs, too.

The evangelist who just talks and talks won't, in the end, be effective because almost no one finds it pleasant just to hear another person talk. A good evangelist *listens*, and through listening makes friends, because friendship is the basis for sharing the highest possible good: the love of God given in the person of Jesus Christ.

James used to think that evangelization meant knowing all the answers, ready to launch into a well-rehearsed speech at a moment's notice. He'd try to steer conversations toward faith, often feeling frustrated when people's eyes glazed over or they quickly changed the subject. His messages, however well-intentioned, felt like arrows shot into the dark, rarely hitting their mark. It was all talk, no connection.

Then, James met an older mentor who showed him a different way. He learned the power of listening—truly listening—to people's stories, their joys, and their struggles. He started focusing on building genuine friendships, finding common ground, and sharing life with others, not just his beliefs. As he invested in these relationships, he found that opportunities to share his faith arose naturally, rooted in trust and mutual respect. Instead of a distant, impersonal sermon, his sharing became a heartfelt conversation, an invitation to explore a relationship with God, not a demand to accept a doctrine. He realized that the gospel wasn't meant to be imposed, but gently offered, person-to-person, heart-to-heart. This shift transformed his approach, making his efforts far more effective and deeply fulfilling.

5

Learn to Listen

We want others to listen to what we have to say about Jesus and his Church, and it is perfectly fair for us to want that. But how can we ask people to listen to us if we have not first listened to them? As Jesus himself said, "Do to others as you would have them do to you" (Luke 6:31).

For this reason, listening isn't a mere gimmick or trick. It isn't the thing we get out of the way so we can move on to what we really want to do. When we listen attentively, we are following the direct command of Christ. And, beyond just following a command, we are *imitating* him. Jesus engaged in countless varied conversations with others even though he was their Creator. He did not simply pronounce to them in a monologue, even though it was his right; he didn't think it a waste of his time to listen to what lowly mortals had to say.

Even in time-constrained situations where it is clear you are not about to become best friends, you can be *friendly;* you can move the relationship onto friendly terms. If you let others know you have heard them and you can relate to

 Cultivate the Lord's peace in your heart and let that peace be your first witness.

them, agreeing with them wherever you can, this creates a bond. You can also show compassion toward them about any difficult situations they're going through; you can be joyful about the good things; and you can, when appropriate, present moral or religious challenges where they are needed. All of this is an imitation of what Jesus did.

The Duty to Proclaim

Just one more thing before we get into specific techniques for listening and befriending: though these steps are essential, they are not the whole process.

It is necessary to say this in order to correct an error that many modern Christians have been taught about evangelization: that you should primarily do it *without words*. Countless Catholics have been told by catechists and pastors that it is best just to treat others with kindness, show the gospel by example, and only get around to talking about Jesus when it is strictly "necessary" to do so.

This teaching, though popular, is enormously damaging.

Worse, it isn't true; and because it isn't true, it doesn't work.

How many people come to the Faith because Christians are so kind? How many people have given their lives to Jesus because they saw you being nice, asked you why you are so nice, heard you reply that Jesus has saved you, and decided that they want your niceness for themselves?

In fact, the far more common scenario is that those who think Christianity is just about being nice will decide that they're more than capable of being good people all on their own, without Jesus and all that other stuff about sin and repentance.

Not only have generations of Christians been taught this false idea that the best way to communicate the gospel is not to talk about the gospel, but many have also come to believe that living in a modern, pluralistic society requires them to keep silent about their faith. They have internalized the lie that it is impolite or intolerant to talk openly about Jesus as the Son of God. They think that, in our era of "tolerance," the best Christian is a silent Christian.

But the truth is, although it has always been Christian teaching that we should be good neighbors, this teaching has never meant that we should simply blend in and let our Christianity, our faith in Jesus, remain hidden.

In fact, this is one of the issues Pope St. Paul VI dealt with back in 1975 in his great letter on modern evangelization, *Evangelii Nuntiandi*. In this letter he lists some "excuses" we might give for not talking about Jesus, and he explicitly remarks that "too frequently" we hear it said "that to impose a truth, be it that of the gospel, or to impose a way, be it that of salvation," is somehow a violation of "religious liberty."

Pope Paul's response to this objection is nothing short of astonishing in its passion and clarity:

> Is it then a crime against others' freedom to proclaim with joy a good news which one has come to know through the Lord's mercy? And why should only falsehood and error, debasement and pornography have the right to be put before people and often unfortunately imposed on them by the destructive propaganda of the mass media?

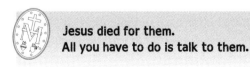

**Jesus died for them.
All you have to do is talk to them.**

Another reason people give for their belief that we modern Catholics should evangelize silently is that the Church, in their view, no longer stresses that the gospel is necessary for salvation. Pope Paul points out, correctly, that many Christians now ask themselves, "Why proclaim the gospel when the whole world is saved by uprightness of heart?"

To these objections, and to the many other objections we modern Catholics sometimes give for our failure to talk openly and confidently about Jesus, Pope Paul answers that "the respectful presentation of Christ and his kingdom is more than the evangelizer's right; it is his duty. It is likewise the right of his fellow men to receive from him the proclamation of the good news of salvation."

Strong words.

Not only do Christians in a pluralistic society have a right to share Jesus—every person on Earth has the right *to hear about* Jesus. We are, in a sense, violating their rights if we are stingy about sharing the gospel with them.

One of the most famous stories illustrating this right to hear the gospel is given to us in the life of Alessandro Serenelli, an attempted rapist and murderer. We might want to dismiss him as unworthy of the gospel, but Christ died for him, and that means Christ's salvation is available to him.

It was, in fact, the girl he murdered, understanding her duty to love others and help them to salvation, who made sure that this violent and unjust man received the fullness of the gospel.

At twenty years old, Alessandro was poor, uneducated, and deeply troubled. He was used to violence, and when he became desirous of an eleven-year-old girl, he attempted to rape her. She resisted, and he stabbed her.

As she lay dying, she forgave him and said, "I want him to be with me in heaven."

Alessandro was sentenced to thirty years in prison and remained unrepentant for a long time. But then something changed. After several years, he had a dream in which the girl appeared to him. That moment broke through his hardened heart. He began to repent, and his behavior changed so dramatically that he was released three years early.

No one would have blamed that young girl—now St. Maria Goretti—if she had refused to forgive and to actively seek salvation for Alessandro. But she did forgive, and even from beyond the grave she sought him out. Alessandro later became a lay Franciscan and lived the rest of his life in a monastery, working as a gardener and porter. He died in 1970, having spent decades in quiet penance and prayer.

Wherever people are in life, and whatever they have done, Christ has a good and holy life to give them. How profound is our duty to let them know this.

Of course, the idea that everyone has the right to hear the gospel is not meant to frighten us into some kind of manic effort. We are not meant to be anxious that we are violating the rights of others when we rest or pray or go to work. Rather, St. Paul VI speaks of this right so that we will understand that the whole Church must move with energy and freedom to see that others have what they need, and not just food, clothing, and other material things.

Each person has a right to these goods, but an even greater right to the spiritual goods of the gospel. Just as the Church must feed the poor and clothe the naked, it must proclaim the gospel to every soul. Any law that prevents this is not merely unjust to the Church, but to all those who have not yet encountered the Church. Any indifference that keeps us from this is not just a personal quirk, but an offense against those still outside the household of God.

Rekindling Evangelistic Zeal

If this offends us as Catholics, if we are reluctant to accept that we have a duty to talk about Jesus because every person we meet has a right to know Jesus, then we must ask not about techniques or methods but about ourselves. Is it possible that we don't truly believe? Have we been so long simmered in the stew of modern agnosticism and relativism that we are no longer sure about the full saving truth of Jesus and his gospel?

Jesus, in the book of Revelation, speaks to the church in Ephesus, commending their hard work and perseverance, but then adding, "Yet I hold this against you: You have forsaken the love you had at first" (2:4). Can the same thing be said of us as individuals? As a Church?

It is frightening to think so, but if others truly have a right to Jesus, how is it that we become nonchalant about that right?

If, in fact, we have grown cold in our love, or have grown too easy-going about salvation, as if everyone just gets it no matter what we do, then we have a problem we need to overcome.

Sometimes we just need a reminder, and perhaps a bit of encouragement, to fan the flames of faith and rekindle our own conviction. In some ways, the whole Church needs this encouragement, every day, so that it will be inspired anew to take up the great work of sharing Jesus, speaking his name to others because they have a right to know him. This zeal

 No matter the outcome they seem to have, bold acts of love are never wasted.

doesn't take root on its own and it doesn't grow without being tended. So, pray for it regularly, and examine yourself regularly to make sure that what you thought was your polite forbearance hasn't turned into the vice of *accedie*—an indifference to spiritual things.

Today's evangelist must understand, yes, that evangelization is not *just* a matter of proclaiming the good news. We can't just stand on street corners shouting. But even more dangerous is the opposite extreme idea: that evangelization is just a matter of listening and befriending and providing witness. And so, we must fight at the same time against two opposite temptations: the temptation to turn evangelization into merely talking about Jesus, and the temptation to turn evangelization into doing everything *except* talking about Jesus.

Evangelization requires *both* listening and speaking, witness and proclamation, because it is a *fully human* act that involves fully human relationships. It begins with hearing what another person has to say and moves to building bridges of friendship. In an open, respectful, and honest way it then moves to proclaiming Jesus and making an invitation to come to him in the sacraments and the life of the Church.

Not all acts of evangelization, of course, will involve all these steps. But, if we master these steps, and seek to employ them, we will be ready.

Ann believed that sharing her faith started with truly listening to others, just as she'd want to be listened to. She strove to be like Jesus, the Creator of everything who still took the time for personal conversations with all sorts of people. Ann knew that even in brief encounters, like at the grocery store or waiting in line, she could build bridges of friendship. She also understood that although being kind and living a good example were important, truly effective evangelization required speaking directly about Jesus.

Some Christians might hesitate, worried about seeming impolite or intolerant, but Ann firmly believed that every person had a right to hear about Jesus, and she knew it was her duty, and every Christian's, duty to share him.

6

Open with Faith

Consider a scenario:

You're taking a plane trip. As everyone is buckling in, you say hello to the person next to you. He has a sweatshirt on from Ohio State University. You used to live in Ohio, so you chat about life in the Buckeye State. You ask about his family. He's got a couple of kids. You've got kids. You share stories. A friendly and relaxed conversation follows about sports, the weather, work, and so on. Then you interject something like, "I'd like to tell you about Jesus . . ."

You listened. You built bridges of friendship. Now you are proclaiming the gospel. This is effective evangelization, right?

But how does all this feel to *him*? Is your seat neighbor now ready for an open and respectful conversation about the Faith?

The truth is, we cannot know. Maybe he had been wanting to talk with someone about Jesus and you arrived just at the right moment. Maybe he had never given much thought to Jesus, but when you said the Lord's name his heart opened, and he now finds he does want to hear what you have to say. Anything is possible.

But is it also possible that as soon as you say the name of Jesus, he feels tricked? Is it possible that he thought you were just having an amiable chat, but now that you turned so suddenly to talk about Jesus he will see your all your friendliness as fake? Is it possible that he will even feel that he has been trapped?

Okay. Now consider another scenario:

You're taking a plane trip. As everyone is buckling in, you say hello to the person next to you. He has a sweatshirt on from Ohio State University. You used to live in Ohio, so you chat about life in the Buckeye State.

Then you say something like, "I carry these medals in my pocket, and I give them out to people I meet. They're called Miraculous Medals, and many Catholics wear them. I'd like to give you this one."

He looks at the medal and says, "Okay. Thanks. But what am I supposed to do with it?"

"You can wear it, or keep it in your pocket, whatever you want. It is mostly just a reminder that God loves you and he's here to help you."

"I'm not Catholic, though."

"Are you a Christian?"

"I was raised a Baptist, but we go to a non-denominational church."

"You prefer that?"

"Mostly. It's a nice community, the people are great."

"As a Baptist, you must have grown up really knowing your Bible . . ."

In this scenario, you know you can talk about Jesus with him, and about the Bible, because he is a practicing Christian. Although we can't know for sure how he feels about

 Every soul matters. Every conversation counts. Every word has a chance to take root.

this conversation, you have been open and honest about your intentions from the moment you offered the gift of the Miraculous Medal, which he accepted and even asked about.

In this scenario, you offered a gift that made clear right from the start that you are a Catholic and you take your faith seriously. In giving the gift, you got to proclaim a little bit of the gospel—that God loves you and is here to help you.

Now, as the conversation continues, you can listen to what your seatmate has to say, and you can build bridges of friendship without having to wait for the moment to "pounce" with the name of Jesus. You have made your intentions clear from the beginning, and for this reason he got a say in whether he wanted to talk about religious faith.

In some cases, this person might refuse the medal and make clear he is not open to a religious conversation. In other cases, you will get other reactions.

As it happens, this person seems to feel that he has been approached honestly and seems willing to converse. Maybe, more conversation will now follow in which more of the Catholic faith can be shared. Maybe in a minute he'll put on his headphones and go to sleep.

At the very least, he now has a Miraculous Medal, a reminder of God's love, and the opportunity to hear from a Catholic about the fullness of the Faith, which, of course, matters because the Church is, itself, the "household of God" (1 Tim. 3:15), and thus the means for encounter with Christ. Ultimately, what the evangelist wants for every person (from the atheist to the non-Catholic Christian to the non-practicing Catholic) is to know Christ and receive him in the sacraments and life of his Church.

Making your intentions clear from the beginning created a certain freedom for both of you. He can decide if he wants to talk with you about religion, and you can talk about it honestly, knowing that you are not sneaking in Jesus or Catholicism on an unsuspecting person.

This is of fundamental importance. Everything we do as evangelists must be open, respectful of the other, and honest. We are not looking just to put another notch in our evangelist belt. We don't want to treat people merely as targets. And so, when we start our conversations, by listening to what others have to say and trying to build bridges of friendship, our usual practice should be to make clear very early that we want to share Jesus.

Or consider a family situation in which you want to invite a relative to consider the Catholic faith. In such a situation, we can become pests if we are constantly trying to insert religion into conversations and situations where it feels like we are ambushing, or maybe even criticizing, our loved ones. We must remember that it is not our job to make sure another person responds to Jesus by embracing the life of faith. Our duty is to proclaim and invite.

What if, instead of potentially harming normal relationships by being *that relative* who constantly introduces religious topics even when they are unwelcome, we took the time to build love and trust by consistently listening and being good to the other person?

Perhaps then we might one day say something like, "Could I have ten minutes of your time this weekend just to tell you what I believe? It is important to me, and I would like to share it. I don't need you to do anything, and I promise I won't go over ten minutes. I just want to share this part of my life with you because you are important to me, but that's all. I just want you to know this part of my life."

It might be that the person will say no, but is that likely if you have truly been attentive and responsive without being pushy? And even if the person does say no, you have done what you could, you still have friendship with the person, and perhaps another opportunity will come in time.

On the other hand, if the person says yes, you have not ambushed him or come at him in an annoying way, and that means you now have an opportunity to proclaim the gospel to one who is, at the very least, going to give you a polite hearing.

You have not treated a person merely as a target. Instead, you have built a personal friendship. Such friendship might just be the bridge over which the truth of the gospel can now travel.

The Jews who gathered in Jerusalem for Pentecost and heard the preaching of Peter and the other apostles were so moved that they asked, "What shall we do?" (Acts 2:37). They knew the gospel message called for some kind of response, and they wanted to know how to make that response.

For the gospel to be effective, it must move from being merely information. The person who receives it must take action. For the person who has not yet taken such action, or maybe who has fallen back into laxity, we must make an *invitation* to action. We must help them make a response. Maybe that will mean inviting the person to return to the sacraments, or simply to prayer, or to make moral changes. Because the gospel message calls for a response, when the time is right, it is the evangelist's job to make the invitation.

7

Try Icebreakers

The gift of a Miraculous Medal in the previous chapter is an example of an *evangelization icebreaker*. When you give someone such a gift, you're not back-dooring him into an evangelization conversation. Instead, you're approaching him with a friendly, upfront signal that you want to talk about faith. People usually like getting gifts. And as a bonus, you usually get instant feedback about whether the person is going to be receptive.

For example, one experienced evangelist was at a home improvement store and offered the cashier a Miraculous Medal. She gasped, grabbed the medal, and clutched it to her chest. She then made the sign of the cross.

Without the woman saying anything to the evangelist, she made clear that she was Catholic and that she was going to be open to a faith message. Because of her reaction to the medal, the evangelist said, "Do you need a miracle in your life for anything?"

Here, in just a matter of seconds, the first two steps of the evangelization process are already accomplished. The evangelist can listen to this person's quite demonstrative reception of the medal, get a sense from this response that this person is in need, and respond as a friend.

She started to cry. Happily, there was no one else in line, so he had a few minutes to talk to her. She wasn't going to Mass, and she was having a hard time with family. The evangelist was able to have an extended conversation in which he was able to encourage her and share with her why getting to Mass and praying were important, why Jesus wanted to meet her there.

Remember, in the broadest sense evangelization is not just about sharing the gospel with unbelievers. Among the most common people you'll meet in the evangelization field are those who have been given the Catholic faith, who may once have practiced the Faith, but who have, in the busyness, messiness, and temptation of modern life, let it go. Jesus has many gifts he wants to shower on such people, chief among them communion with him in the sacraments. These are the very sheep that the Good Shepherd says he goes out in search of, and he assures us that he rejoices over them when they are found.

Later, reflecting on this fruitful and friendly encounter, the evangelist said, "I didn't do anything. The Miraculous Medal did it."

This sentiment is common among evangelists who use gifts as icebreakers. A well-chosen gift communicates a message all on its own. Frequently, the person who receives the gift is ready for a word of encouragement and maybe even an invitation to return to or take up the life of faith in ways the evangelist could not have imagined.

The choice of an icebreaker is up to the evangelist, and it can be connected to the personal message the evangelist has already crafted. Some common icebreakers include rosaries,

A small gift like the Miraculous Medal might be the seed that blooms into salvation.

holy cards, saint medals, and books. In the case of the Miraculous Medal, one of the messages this evangelist had crafted was expressed in the question, "Do you need a miracle in your life for anything?"

This question didn't just drop from the sky but was one of the messages the evangelist had ready. If, for example, the person had said, "I'm a Christian, and I don't believe in magical medals," the evangelist might have followed with something more Bible-based, perhaps, "I agree with you that Christians should not be involved in magic, but even the apostles used religious objects, like St. Paul's handkerchiefs in Acts 19."

What might have followed then would have been a conversation about how the Bible, in many places, teaches the use of religious objects, and how the Catholic Church has kept that teaching alive.

Or what if the person had simply said, "No thanks, I don't believe in God"? Well, the evangelist would have a crafted message for that, as well.

Icebreakers are not always necessary. Sometimes other openings present themselves, especially with people who you already have relationships with. But, certainly for anyone who wants to make a habit of evangelization, having an icebreaker available will prove helpful.

Opening Doors

Not all icebreakers are physical items. The person who makes the sign of the cross in public before eating is giving a momentary witness to others that might occasion a conversation. Some people break the ice simply by asking others, at appropriate times, if they have anything they would like to have the evangelist pray about. At a restaurant, it is common for Catholics to say grace before eating, but some go so far as to mention to the waitress, "We are about to say grace, is there anything you would like us to pray for?" Sometimes a phrase as simple as "God bless you" can also break the ice with someone.

The use of icebreakers isn't strictly necessary, but they allow the evangelist to introduce faith in a way that doesn't trap the other person or make the other person feel put upon. In addition, such gifts generally bring a verbal response. If the evangelist is a willing listener, that response will give important information about where the person is in the spiritual life and whether the person is interested in a conversation about faith.

Also, many religious objects are also *sacramentals*. This means they have spiritual power to aid in sharing Jesus. As the *Catechism* reminds us, sacramentals prepare people "to receive the fruit of the sacraments and sanctify different circumstances of life" (1677). The use of sacramentals in evangelization, then, is more than a conversation-starter strategy. It fosters the action of grace by reminding us and others of the presence of the holy. They quite literally bring holiness into everyday moments. Both the evangelist and the person receiving the gift can benefit from the "sanctification" sacramentals provide. When we use them, we ask the help of heaven, and we can be confident we receive it. We are not alone in the evangelizing task. Rather, we are surrounded by those who help us in our efforts, including Jesus, himself.

Saint Maximilian Kolbe, most famous for having given his life in exchange for another prisoner in the Nazi concentration camp at Auschwitz, used to call the Miraculous Medal "Our Lady's Silver Bullet." This brilliant writer and thinker was as humble as a child in his love for the Miraculous Medal, giving many away because he believed just coming into possession of such a medal might bring the miraculous conversion of any person.

He particularly loved the story of the conversion of Alphonse Ratisbonne, who became a Catholic priest despite having harbored a deep, and quite vocal, anti-Catholicism. Jewish by birth but not religious, Ratisbonne found himself, through unlikely circumstances, among a circle of Catholic friends in Rome. They gave him a Miraculous Medal to wear, prayed for his conversion, and offered sacrifices for him. One day, waiting for one of these friends inside a Catholic church, he had a vision of the Blessed Virgin. She did not speak to him, but, appearing just as she looks on the Miraculous Medal, she wordlessly conveyed her love for him and the truth of the Catholic faith.

Kolbe, whom Pope John Paul II once referred to as the "patron" of the twentieth century, took great inspiration from such stories. Recent decades have seen a wave of revival among Catholics undertaking direct evangelization, and, again and again, the Miraculous Medal has played an important role. It was central, for example, to the founding of St. Paul Street Evangelization, and remains the primary item used by the group for breaking the ice and inviting conversations about the Faith.

Many kinds of icebreaker items have something to recommend them. For someone just starting out in evangelization, however, the Miraculous Medal can reasonably be considered the best option. It is beautiful but small, and lots

That medal, card, or cross might be the first sacramental someone has ever touched.

of them can fit in a pocket. It has a wonderful story. It can be given on a chain to be worn around the neck or just placed as a token in the hand.

We can have confidence in the Miraculous Medal because the Mother of God, in her own words, called for us to have confidence. In 1830, she appeared to St. Catherine Laboure and gave her the design for the medal. Our Lady explained that in using the medal and praying the prayer that goes with it, "Graces will be abundantly bestowed upon those who have confidence."

This appearance of Mary, coming in France just at the moment it did, was clearly meant as a divine help especially intended for modern people. At that time, the modern world as we understand it was being born. France had been rocked by a series of secular revolutions that had seen the murder of countless faithful Catholics, the destruction of whole networks of Catholic institutions, and widespread, violent attacks on priests and religious. The old Catholic world was giving way to the new secular world, and it was a merciless transition. Soon France would fall under the sway of the great man, Napoleon, who vacillated between protecting and demonizing the Church as he mobilized the whole of society for horrifying new kinds of war under the banner of nationalism.

All the while, the Industrial Revolution was beginning to transform every aspect of society. The former rural life was passing away, being replaced by the life of factory work and great cities. However much they were told they would enjoy the benefits of "modernization," the people of this new world would be spiritually devastated, becoming, generation by generation, the most anxious, dislocated, and confused people the world has ever known.

It was for these people—those of us who live now in a

rich, busy, self-centered, and lonely world—that the Miraculous Medal was given as a token of God's intimate love for each and every soul. If the world was to separate us from one another and isolate us as lonely individuals, the Mother of God was going to remind us that we still belonged in the family of God; that each of us still had an important place in his plan and mattered deeply to him.

The Miraculous Medal was given by a loving mother through the humblest of religious sisters. In this way, it reminds us of the Incarnation of Christ, who entered a violent and broken world in the humblest way in order to have the most humanizing effect. The mother of Jesus gave us this gift for the very purpose of bringing the good news that each modern person most needs: the news that the God of love has not forgotten you.

When we open conversations by giving Miraculous Medals, or by using any other faith-centered icebreakers, we treat the other person with respect, both giving them a gift and an opportunity to talk about God. Far from trapping them in conversations they don't want, we merely try to create openings for conversations in which we can offer what we have been given: the love of God in Jesus Christ.

Rich had a knack for starting conversations. He'd often offer a Miraculous Medal to people he met. These small tokens were gentle invitations, bridging the gap for those who had drifted from their faith. For Rich, it wasn't just about the medal itself, but the spiritual significance it carried, a quiet prayer that the sacramental would open hearts and prepare them to receive God's grace, drawing them back to a faith they once knew.

8
Hone the Skill of Friendship

How do I know when another person is truly my friend? Most of us would answer something like, "When another person knows me and loves me, I know he is my friend."

When I know that someone knows me and loves me, I can let down my guard. I can trust. I can be myself, talk freely, and share ideas without feeling defensive.

This is the kind of conversation we want to have with people about the Catholic faith. Our interest is to remove obstacles to the reception of the gospel. Defensiveness, fear, antagonism, and mistrust are all obstacles that we can remove by befriending the other person. Wherever we can, we want to plant the seed of the gospel, and what better place to plant it than in a heart that is open to a word from a friend?

If we are willing, we can learn to have conversations with other people, even strangers, in which they can be themselves with us, talk freely, and share ideas because they know

 it may sound like a small thing, but don't underestimate the power of a simple invitation to prayer.

we are not against them, but for them.

Such conversations are ennobling rather than demeaning. Because they respect the dignity of the human person, they are uplifting rather than discouraging. These conversations, in which people are allowed to let down their guard and talk honestly, are also consistent with Christian love. How else would the Lord, who instructed us to love others as he loved us, want us to treat another person?

Some people have a natural talent for befriending others. They are effortlessly able to put others at ease and can build rapport even with strangers. This kind of talent can be a genuine aid to evangelization. But many good, kind, and faithful people don't have—or, at least, don't feel they have—an abundance of this talent. Such people might well be filled with the Spirit and truly willing to evangelize. But are they able?

The answer is that *each* of us, no matter our natural gifts or lack thereof, can learn and practice the skills required to befriend other people. And there is no shortage of help. Within the Church, groups such as St. Paul Street Evangelization, the Legion of Mary, the Fellowship of Catholic University Students, and many others are ready to help people build up these skills. Books, courses, and conferences on evangelization, catechesis, and ministry can help. And, today, there are countless Catholic media resources—websites, podcasts, television and radio outlets—that offer opportunities to gain confidence in methods for sharing the Faith. Evangelization is not meant to be a lonely pursuit, but one that the whole Catholic community takes on together.

Beyond the Soapbox

The human person is a great mystery; and one of the most mysterious things we do is enter into friendship.

Whole volumes have been devoted just to the meaning of the word *friendship*. And there are probably countless kinds and levels of friendship. But, in general, when we speak of befriending others as part of evangelization, we are talking about removing competition and antagonism while *coming alongside persons*, making clear that we are for them and not against them. Christianity is a shared life.

This should not make us think that evangelization can only be done when the evangelist has lots of time. If a person masters the skills of breaking the ice with others, asking engaging questions, and listening carefully, even in a grocery line there can be time enough to converse, listen, share, and at least plant a seed of the gospel—maybe even invite the person to take positive steps toward Jesus and the Church.

People chat in grocery lines all the time about the weather or the news. If you are one of those grocery-line chatters, doing evangelization while in line might just involve adding some specific references to the gospel to what you already do. If you tend to avoid conversation at such times, it might be harder for you, but with a little instruction you may well find you like it. And don't worry if the thought striking up a grocery-line conversation just horrifies you. You can apply the same techniques in situations that are more natural for you.

 The Holy Spirit is more interested in your availability than your ability.

Here's how it might go:

You, meeting the eye of the person in front of you in line: "Hello."

Person in front of you in line: "Hi."

You: "I carry these medals in my pocket, and I give them out to people, and it is just on my heart to give you one. Have you ever heard of the Miraculous Medal? I'd love to give you this one if you'd like it."

Person: "Oh, my mother used to have one of those, or something like it, but to be honest, I don't really know anything about that kind of stuff."

You: "It was given to a Catholic nun about 200 years ago in a vision. Many people report miracles and blessings when they wear one. You were raised Catholic?"

Person: "Yes, but I don't really go to church."

You: "Well, if you'd like, here is the medal and a little card that explains it."

Person: "Thank you."

You: "I go to the 10 a.m. Sunday Mass at St. Mary's. Have you ever thought about coming back?"

Person: "I never really got a lot out of it."

You: "I understand. I stayed away for a long time myself. But now it keeps me close to God."

The line moves. The person in front of you turns to the cashier and becomes busy with bagging and paying.

"Nice talking with you," you say as the person begins to leave. "Maybe I'll see you at St. Mary's sometime."

The person smiles and gives you a little wave as you turn to the cashier.

Here, in this little encounter, even though it isn't a perfect encounter, and even though it does not produce any miraculous result, we see some of the basic methods involved in planting the seed of the gospel.

It is a friendly, open, and honest exchange. Using the

Miraculous Medal as an icebreaker, the evangelist has found a non-threatening way to open a conversation about faith. This gesture elicits the response that the person had a Catholic mother.

The evangelist has already crafted a message for lukewarm or fallen-away Catholics, so if this conversation were to continue, say, into the parking lot, the evangelist is ready to present reasons to return to the full practice of the Faith.

Note that the evangelist doesn't just launch into a "pitch" to return to Mass. Instead, the evangelist asks, "You were raised Catholic?"

The person in line is, like everyone else on this planet, on a journey. The evangelist wants to hear whatever the person would like to say about that journey. Some people will say something like (and this really happens), "I have not been to Mass in decades, but it is so weird that you would ask me because I have been thinking I want to go back." Other people might say (and this, too, happens), "I'm really not interested in talking about religion."

Either way, the evangelist has made the overture. The evangelist has done what Jesus calls us to do.

As it happens, this person has a Catholic background but never really got anything out of going to Mass. Here, because the evangelist has listened, the evangelist is able to build a bridge of friendship by expressing understanding rooted in shared experience, *"I understand. I stayed away for a long time myself."*

Later we will talk about proclaiming the gospel and making an invitation as part of the process of talking with others about Jesus. In this instance, you see some proclamation of the gospel in a personal way when the evangelist talks about the Mass with this non-practicing Catholic: "It keeps me close to God."

This little vignette shows what can be accomplished in a very short time. Because this evangelist does not take on the burden of "converting" anyone or trying to be the ultimate savior of anyone's soul, but simply tries to plant the seed of faith, this interaction is relaxed, friendly, and potentially—we really can't know for sure—fruitful. At least we know the person in the grocery line left with a Miraculous Medal, a little card describing the medal, a reminder that closeness to God can be found at Mass, and a specific invitation to come to Mass.

Listening and being open to friendship are not so hard. They can even be fun.

It is charity—which we might define as Christlike love—that unites all the Church's efforts, whether feeding the hungry, visiting the prisoner, or sharing the gospel in a grocery line. So long as we are truly people who love God and neighbor and who share the gospel because we want our neighbor to possess God, we can be humble in our evangelizing. We can let other people have their say, build bridges of friendship, and trust the Holy Spirit to do the work of conversion so that we can focus merely on making friends and planting seeds.

As she became more experienced as an evangelist, Maria came to understand that genuine friendship held the key to breaking down walls of fear, defensiveness, and mistrust. But it didn't happen overnight. Whereas some people seemed to be natural at making friends, for Maria it took work. She was confident, however, that it was a skill anyone could develop with enough practice and guidance, and in time she developed an ease with people that rivaled any extrovert's.

Maria championed a simple, relational approach to evangelization, focusing on making people feel invited rather than pressured. For her, the goal was always to make friends and simply share the gospel, trusting God completely with the outcome. In this she was bolstered by reminding herself often that sharing faith, when done humbly and kindly, was just as profound an act of love as feeding the hungry or visiting the sick.

9

Prepare Your Reasons

Try this. Ask your computer to translate the word *reason* into Greek.

It will give you the word *logos*.

Then consider this ancient scriptural description of Jesus as the Son of God:

> In the beginning was the [*Logos*], and the [*Logos*] was with God, and the [*Logos*] was God. He was in the beginning with God. All things came into being through him, and without him not one thing came into being . . . And the [*Logos*] became flesh and lived among us (John 1: 1-4,14).

Now, "reason" is not the only meaning of *logos*. It also means "word," which is how Christians translate it most often when it is used in the Bible to refer to Jesus. But the fact that *logos*, the word used to describe the Son of God through whom all things were made, includes "reason" as part of its definition, makes clear to us how close to the heart of God "reason" is.

Christianity is, truly, the most reasonable thing in the world. Its setting is within history. It isn't a religion of myths that take place in imaginary lands, but of real people in real places. Right amidst the great civilizations of the world, God reveals himself. And his revelation is testable. People can read the records, investigate the claims, dig up the ancient lands and see what they find. And what is more, this revelation has proven itself again and again by producing saints who could call people out of sin and corruption, healing individuals and sometimes bringing whole societies out of darkness. This revelation presents humanity with the fullest possible picture of the cause, meaning, and destination of the world.

Christianity, as century after century constantly rediscovers, makes sense, makes the world better, and passes every intellectual and moral test. There is not one bit of Christianity that violates reason or asks its followers to violate reason.

What is more, throughout the Gospels, Jesus is seen reason*ing* with people: answering questions, telling stories, explaining the meanings of Scripture. These are important features of his method as a communicator.

At the very heart of Christianity, then, is the notion that God is reasonable; and because God is reasonable, the call to follow Jesus (God in the flesh) involves not just blind faith but an appeal to reason. In his second letter, the apostle Peter tells us, "For we did not follow cleverly devised myths when we made known to you the power and coming of our Lord Jesus Christ, but we were eyewitnesses of his majesty" (2 Pet. 1:16).

Of course, giving reasons does not mean we can compel people to accept the Faith merely by force of argument. To come to accept Jesus as the Son of God requires faith. Such

No one is ever evangelized by accident. Say something.

faith becomes possible when a person hears what Jesus has said and done, becomes convinced that these things truly happened, and—by a gift of the Holy Spirit—becomes able to accept him as who he claims to be: the Son of God, our Savior.

Our role is to call people to the faith, remove obstacles to belief, and plant seeds so that, humanly speaking, faith has a chance.

Peter famously instructed the earliest Christian believers that if anyone should ask for a reason (*logon*) for their Christian hope, each one should be ready to defend Christianity "with gentleness and reverence" (1 Pet. 3:15). From this instruction we can see that from its earliest days, Christian evangelization has involved *answering questions* and *giving reasons*.

Even as we affirm that faith in Jesus is a supernatural gift of the Holy Spirit, we must also affirm that we have been called to work on behalf of the gospel, to prepare the way for Jesus in the minds and hearts of others, just as John the Baptist did. The Holy Spirit does not merely break into the mind and heart like a robber or a tyrant forcing people to accept God. He allows each of us to decide whether we want the gift of Jesus, whether we want to turn from sin and selfishness to accept the fullness of life offered by Jesus.

Catholic evangelists merely cooperate with the Holy Spirit. When we give reasons for belief and we invite others to accept Jesus, we join in the work of turning hearts toward God so that they can receive the gift of faith.

This is why we give reasons for the Christian hope we carry within us, so that others can overcome obstacles, let go of objections, listen to the Spirit, and choose God, if they want him. We are there to be channels of grace and ambassadors for Christ. As his ambassadors, we follow his example in giving reasons.

For example, when John the Baptist sent disciples to Jesus asking if he was the Messiah, Jesus didn't rebuke the question. He didn't demand blind faith. He gave reasons for John's disciples to believe: "The blind receive their sight, the lame walk, the lepers are cleansed, the deaf hear, the dead are raised, and the poor have good news brought to them" (Matt. 11:5).

The Gospel writers present Jesus as one who seemingly every day gave signs of his identity by performing miracles, fulfilling prophecies, and teaching with authority. He also gave signs of his love by healing the sick, casting out demons, and raising the dead. Thus, he made clear both who he is (Messiah and Lord) and what he has come to do for us—to give us life abundantly (John 10:10).

Reasons for Your Hope

Communicating reasons for faith is at the very heart of evangelization. Our hope is that in the light of reasons given, hearts and minds may welcome the movement of the Holy Spirit prompting them to freely choose Jesus, to repent, to believe the Good News of the Kingdom of God, and to take up the devout life.

Here we must always keep in mind Peter's words about maintaining a spirit of "gentleness and reverence" as we share our reasons. Most especially, we must be gentle with persons while maintaining proper reverence for the truth.

The person to whom we are speaking has a dignity that

Invite others not just to believe, but to receive especially in the sacraments.

we must not offend, on the one hand, by being pushy, deceptive, or otherwise ill-mannered. Likewise, because of the dignity of the person to whom we are speaking, we must not water down the truth or withhold the fullness of the gospel.

Unfortunately, many people who deeply desire to share Jesus lose their confidence when they are reminded that they must give reasons for their Christian hope. Many feel they are not up to this task. How many people, even though they wanted to talk about Jesus with another person, have held their tongue because they didn't feel they had the right words, or didn't feel they knew enough theology to make a good case for Jesus?

One thought that can get us back on track when we feel this way about our own abilities is to remember that Jesus called us to this work *knowing our limitations*, just as he called Peter to this work knowing his. If he could say to the great apostle Paul, "My grace is sufficient for you, for my power is made perfect in weakness" (2 Cor.12:9), how much more must those words apply to us?

Although this thought that God wants us to share the gospel—that he has chosen us for this work—should give us confidence, however, it should not blind us to the reality that we must *prepare*. Peter did not say to "just get out there and do it." We must be ready.

From his own experience of long apprenticeship with Jesus, Peter knew that preparation makes all the difference. The message he gave when filled with the Holy Spirit on Pentecost, for example, wasn't something he just dreamed up. He had spent three years learning it directly from the Master himself. What the Holy Spirit gave was the recollection of the message and the power to share it fearlessly.

Like Peter, we can learn the reasons for faith and practice them. We can be ready with them so that, when the moment comes for the proclamation of the gospel, we will have something to proclaim.

Jan was never one for demanding blind faith. She understood that Christianity wasn't about shutting off your brain but engaging it. The Jesus she knew from Scripture always answered questions and even performed miracles as evidence for himself.

When Jan shared her faith, she saw her role as clearing the path for others. She patiently answered questions and offered compelling reasons for belief, knowing that true conversion was ultimately God's work, not hers. She cooperated with the Holy Spirit, never forcing, always respecting human freedom. And though she trusted completely in God's grace, she also knew that being a good evangelist meant continually studying, learning, and practicing how to articulate the hope within her.

10

Give
"One Good Reason"

Years of trial and error at St. Paul Street Evangelization have yielded a particularly effective method to prepare people for the proclamation of the gospel. They call it the *One Good Reason Method*, and it represents the core of what we would like to convey in this book.

As one might expect from the name, this method aims to prepare each of us as an evangelist to share one good reason for our own faith in Christ, and to do so in a way that is helpful to the person we have already listened to and befriended.

In the course of an honest and friendly conversation, one in which we have made clear to the other person that we want to talk about Jesus, we will get a sense, first of all, of whether the person is open to such a conversation, and if so, where the person is on his own journey of faith. This is where listening to others gives us a great advantage: at the moment of proclaiming the gospel, we can share the message that most seems to fit for the person.

Perhaps we get a sense that this person already has a relationship with Jesus, for example, and is fully living the life of sacraments and charity in the Catholic Church. For such a person we might simply offer an invitation to read a certain helpful book or join a particular ministry; or, we might just offer words of encouragement to help him persevere in the Faith, perhaps inviting him to pray for us as evangelists. *One good reason* to go deeper.

Maybe we find the person is already fully committed to Jesus but isn't Catholic. We might ask such a person, *"Can I give you one good reason why I am a Catholic?"*

Notice that this question is carefully crafted. It is formulated to respect the other person's right to say, "No thank you." However, it is also formulated to decrease the likelihood that the other person will say, "No thank you."

First, it is only going to be one reason—not a long speech or argument. This eases the anxiety many people have that they will be trapped in a long conversation they don't want. Second, you are not telling the other person what he should do. You are asking if you can tell *your* reason for doing what *you* do.

Third, by promising a "good" reason you are engaging the other person's curiosity. What could this good reason be?

If you were instead to ask, "Can I tell you why I think you should be Catholic?" the effect would be quite different. This question would neither reassure the person that you are going to be brief nor raise his curiosity. Worst of all, it would do the one thing almost no one likes—tell him what he should do. People naturally resist this. To tell another person what he should do is to put him on the defensive and invite argument.

 You don't need an academic degree to evangelize. You just need a love for souls.

Instead, in the One Good Reason Method, we share our own experience . . . and it's hard to argue with another person's experience. This means that we are likely to open avenues of conversation rather than close them off. And if our reason is succinct and well prepared it has a chance of being effective. Rather than droning on and on, we can get directly to the point and share the message we hoped to share.

After that, anything might happen.

Here's how that might go in the case of the person who is already Christian but not Catholic:

"Can I give you one good reason why I am Catholic?"

"All right."

"Jesus said, 'Be perfect as your Father in heaven is perfect,' and I realized that I could not do it. I came to see that I could not overcome my moral faults, my doubts, or my spiritual laziness. So why did Jesus command us to be perfect as the Father is if we cannot do it? Well, for a lot of reasons, I started to go to the church and sit quietly with Jesus in the sacrament. After I would receive communion, I would just sit with him and talk. Sometimes I just sat quietly for a long time not knowing what to say.

"Over time, I realized that the sacrament was working on me. Jesus was really there, and he was healing me, giving me strength to overcome my moral faults, my doubts, and even my spiritual laziness. I became more peaceful, less grumpy, and more charitable toward other people. I have never found anything with the power to change me in that way.

"Now I just want to share Jesus with other people. I want them to come to him in the Eucharist, at the Mass, and be healed by him.

"He said, 'I am the living bread which came down from heaven; if anyone eats of this bread, he will live forever,' and I know that in the Catholic Church I can receive this bread every day. I know it really gives eternal life."

What will the other person make of reason? We can't know for sure, but neither should we be overly concerned. If we are ambassadors for Christ and the fullness of his truth, we are there to give the message, not to determine the outcome. If we are seed-planters, we must be content to plant the seed and leave the rest in the hands of the Holy Spirit.

This evangelist was able to listen to another person and offer a gospel truth in a way that was tailored to this. He has shared the good news of Jesus Christ as the bread of life who is available every day in every Catholic Church.

That is enough. If the conversation ends here, fine. If it goes on for another hour and then later they meet for coffee a few times, and later the person comes to Mass to see what it is all about, also fine!

Some other questions the evangelist might ask, depending on the other person's situation, include:

Can I give you one good reason why I choose to believe in God?

Can I give you one good reason why I choose to put my faith in Jesus?

Can I give you one good reason why I go to Mass?

The One Good Reason Method can be adapted to each person without short-changing the fullness of the gospel message. For example, the atheist who has never encountered a "good reason" to believe in God will be entirely closed off from accepting Jesus or the Catholic Church. Once we know this, we can decide how to proceed. For some atheists, depending on their reasons for atheism, we might decide that talk of Jesus or the Church is the place to start. But what if the person signals that he just thinks all this "God stuff" is idiotic and childish?

For such a person, we might speak first of belief in God in the most general way. If he finds our reason for belief in God compelling, new horizons will open. Perhaps this person who always thought of religion as a crutch or a scam can at least begin to see that religious people have reasons for their beliefs. And if there are reasons to believe in God, then just maybe there are reasons to believe in Jesus. Maybe there are even reasons to be baptized and to live the Catholic life of sacraments and charity!

Thus, beginning where the person is and adapting our message to address the real obstacles the person faces is not the same as presenting a false or easy gospel. It is, rather, to start the presentation of the full gospel right where the person is ready to start.

A Framework for Sharing

We began this book by describing the importance of sharing the entire good news/bad news/good news narrative of the gospel. We then described why it is necessary for each evangelist to craft a message. The One Good Reason Method provides a helpful and specific framework for crafting our message so that it is truly our own and it truly speaks to another person. With One Good Reason, even an evangelist who has limited theological training can "be prepared" just as St. Peter instructed. Your reason can be a philosophical or theological reason, or it can be entirely personal. It is your reason, and when you share it, you are sharing the gospel in a personal way.

 Every baptism happens because someone once had courage to speak.

For Matt, the "One Good Reason" technique was a powerful game changer. He didn't need to dazzle people with a comprehensive sermon, but could start simply, with one honed and heartfelt appeal.

When he shared his own good reason for belief, he noticed something remarkable: people listened differently. They didn't feel the need to defend their own views or challenge his, because he was simply sharing his own story, not forcing anything upon them. They didn't think to raise all the objections and accusations about Christianity that they had imbibed from the culture, because Matt's one reason was so focused and so sincere.

Matt firmly believed that adapting the message didn't mean diluting the gospel; the full, rich truth remained intact. In fact, he found that when he shared his unique and personal reason for faith, it made the entire gospel message feel more relatable and real to the person listening.

11

Share the Promise
and the Warning

The Christian message is not merely a promise of light and life—it is also a warning against darkness and sin.

God has a certain way of dealing with us when he wants to get our attention and turn us back to himself. We see his own "method" revealed time and again in Scripture. And after the time of the apostles, as the early Church then spread out into the world, it imitated this method in its own evangelizing. And then, down through the centuries, the great saints and evangelists did the same.

After saving the ancient Hebrew people and giving them his commandments, God tells them, "See, I have set before you this day life and good, death and evil" (Deut. 30:15). He urges them to "choose life, that you and your descendants may live" (Deut. 30:19).

God makes clear to them here—and through countless other means, including the instruction of prophets—that if they choose the path of evil it will lead to accursedness and death, whereas if they choose the path of good it will lead to blessedness and life.

At the center of God's "method" for drawing his people back to goodness, back to love and peace, is both a promise and a warning. So long as they avoid evil and remain close to him, they are safe and all is well. But if they turn back to evil, they put themselves in danger of terrible loss.

Throughout the life of the Church, evangelization has likewise included both the promise and the warning. The Church's great evangelists have set before people two roads: one that leads to life and the other to destruction. This contrast (life vs. death, glory vs. condemnation, happiness vs. despair, salvation vs. damnation) motivated the great evangelists by filling them with zeal to help others avoid destruction, and it formed an important part of their message as they attempted to motivate others to flee from destruction and choose the blessed life.

If we no longer take sin seriously, and if we no longer are concerned that souls can be lost, where will we find the zeal to persevere in evangelizing as the saints did? And if we treat God's method as a thing of the past, refusing in our own evangelization to convey the warning, won't some people refuse to listen, thinking that everything is okay no matter what they do?

In saying this, we are not suggesting that you go out into the street shouting at people about hell. Nor do we think that mere fear-mongering should prevail in homes or schools or parishes. God's method is not one of terrorizing. He sent prophets and saints to share the truth of his mercy. He described himself to Moses as "merciful and gracious, slow to anger, and abounding in steadfast love and faithfulness, keeping steadfast love for the thousandth generation, forgiving

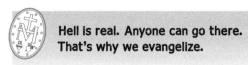

**Hell is real. Anyone can go there.
That's why we evangelize.**

iniquity and transgression and sin" (Exod. 34:6-7). In the New Testament, St. Paul describes God as "our Savior, who desires everyone to be saved and to come to the knowledge of the truth" (1 Tim. 2:3-4).

The whole weight of Scripture impresses us with this message: God loves us, has mercy on us, and wants to fill us with good things. But, to Moses, God also described himself as "by no means clearing the guilty" (Exod. 34:7). And Paul, himself an apostle of mercy, does not hesitate to warn even his fellow Christians against sin; telling the Galatians, for example, that

> the works of the flesh are obvious: fornication, impurity, licentiousness, idolatry, sorcery, enmities, strife, jealousy, anger, quarrels, dissensions, factions, envy, drunkenness, carousing, and things like these. I am warning you, as I warned you before: those who do such things won't inherit the kingdom of God (Gal. 5:19-21).

No, it simply cannot be denied that the Lord's method for reaching people includes the *warning* as well as the *promise*. Jesus' words and actions are, in almost every case, comforting, patient, and healing. His ministry of teaching, healing, and exorcism is aimed entirely at restoration, forgiveness, and peace. But he speaks about damnation more than any other person in Scripture.

While certainly avoiding any hint of sensationalism or theatrics, we must imitate God in this. This desire to imitate him must guide us in the messages we craft. As his was, the far greater portion of our message must be the truth about God's love and mercy. But, also like him, we must not neglect the warning.

Addressing Sin Constructively

To a degree, we covered this idea when we stressed that the fullness of the gospel message involves good news, bad news, and good news. But how do we speak to individual people about the sin that might be keeping them from friendship with God?

First, if we must talk with others about sin, we must do so gently and without condemnation. It is not our role to judge others harshly or brutalize others emotionally. But consider the following encounter of a street evangelist with a person of good will. Though it has the qualities of gentleness and friendliness, it also introduces the idea of sin in a way that might motivate and be helpful to the person:

The evangelist is part of a Saturday morning evangelizing group that has a table set up in a public place. People walk by and see the rosaries, Miraculous Medals, books, and other items on the table. Some ask about what the group is doing. Others pass by at a distance, giving clear signs that they don't want to be disturbed. Still others say hello as they pass.

The evangelist exchanges pleasant hellos with a woman passing. She clearly recognizes that the material is Catholic and comments that she is Catholic but doesn't go to church.

The evangelist could launch right into giving reasons that the woman should return to church, but, instead, she takes an inquisitive approach.

"Was there something that turned you away from going to Mass?"

"Not really. I just learned that I could find God everywhere. I meet him just as much walking on the beach as I ever did in church."

"Oh, the beach is a great place to talk with God. Do you pray as you are walking?"

"I mean, I just know he's there with me."

"I think I understand. And I'm sure you're right. He is there with you. But do you think it is important to live in friendship with God?"

"Yes. I just think you can have friendship with God in a lot of ways."

"I spent years away from going to Mass at one time in my life, but now I love to go to Mass. Can I share with you just one good reason why I went back?"

"Okay, sure."

"A friend pointed out to me that when Jesus instituted the first Mass he said, 'Do this in memory of me.' And that is the only thing he ever commanded us to do in his memory. This is what Jesus wants his friends to do. He also said, 'You are my friends if you keep my commandments.' I realized that if I truly wanted to be his friend, I needed to keep all of his commandments, including this commandment to celebrate the Eucharist in memory of him."

Notice that this conversation didn't include the word *sin* or *hell* or *damnation* or any other such dramatic term. Still, the evangelist was able to convey the idea that we must keep God's commandments. This is the essence of the Christian message about sin: our continued friendship with God depends on keeping his commandments.

As with all the conversational examples in this book, different evangelists might have approached this in different ways. But here you see one example of how evangelization can avoid drama and brimstone without cutting sin, death,

Confession isn't just healing—it's rescue. Invite someone to it.

and loss of friendship with God out of the conversation.

"Is it important to follow God's commandments?"

"If we want to be friends with God, do we have to do what he says?"

Such questions allow us a non-combative way to introduce to modern people the same warning that has always been part of God's revelation, the warning that evil leads to death and loss.

We are not imposing something from outside of the gospel when we remind people of Jesus' own words: "You are my friends if you do what I command you" (John 15:14) That "if" is not an accident. It is a vital part of the proclamation of the true gospel.

In a 1924 article in his magazine, *The Knight of the Immaculata*, St. Maximilian Kolbe said, "The spiritual life is a battle because the eternal destiny of our souls hangs in the balance. God wants us to go to heaven and the devil wants us to go to hell. The battle is over our hearts, to which we alone hold the key. Everything hangs on the choice that we make, and the determination at the end of our lives is absolute, final, and irrevocable. We are either totally victorious or totally destroyed."

We should not be too quick to think that modern people cannot handle this reality. Today, we might not generally use the same words Maximilian used, but we can still fortify people for the battle, get them to accept that there is a battle, and help them find the weapons—primarily prayer, charity, and the sacraments—that will equip them to fight.

"There are no atheists in foxholes," the old battlefield saying goes. A retired Marine, Jorge found success with an approach to evangelization that reminds people, gently but frankly, that the truth is we're *all* in a foxhole. No matter how safe, healthy, and materially comfortable our lives right now, we're all under threat from temptation and sin, and we're all going to die someday. Nobody *wants* to think about this, but almost everyone senses it. To some degree, everyone is aware that he is a sinner and is worried about what will happen after death.

Jorge refined an approach that emphasized God's love and mercy while also helping people to recognize the danger to the souls. He was able to balance the message of God's boundless love with an acknowledgment of the serious consequences of actions that lead us away from him. This is the warning that makes the promise compelling.

Throughout Scripture, there's a clear and consistent presentation of the choice between life and death, blessings and curses (Deut. 30:19). Historically, evangelists have been deeply motivated by the profound reality that sin ultimately leads to destruction. This reality moves them not only to more urgent evangelization but more *effective* evangelization.

PART THREE

Live the Message

12

Be Yourself Converted

Proclaiming the gospel in response to our baptismal call is more than an act, or a technique; it's certainly not "one weird trick" or a game played for souls. Above all, it is a *life*. It changes *who we are* and how we bear ourselves every day.

The basic features of a life of evangelization, the qualities and virtues that this life requires of and builds in us, look something like this:

1) The evangelist must be willing and able to *speak the truth in love*. This person must be clear, kind, and courageous enough to offer the whole truth, the good news and the bad.

2) The evangelist must also be a person who can *persevere*, accepting that rejection, dryness, and discouragement will come and are part of the spiritual battle every evangelist must face.

 Let your life and your bearing radiate your message. Authenticity opens more hearts than perfection ever could.

3) In order to do these things, the evangelist must be

    a) a person *who lives the faith*—because personal holiness gives credibility to our words;

    b) a person of *prayer and sacrifice*— because evangelization is truly God's work and we need to be ready to beg him to prepare hearts just as we need to offer sacrifices for the good of those who will be evangelized; and

    c) a person who *relies on the sacraments*—because there is real supernatural power in the sacraments. Jesus gave them to us for a reason. Our baptism truly makes new creatures of us and makes us members of Christ. The Eucharist truly feeds us spiritually. Confession truly frees us from sin and empowers us to overcome sin.

4) Finally, the evangelist must be a person who *works with others,* because community gives courage and accountability.

If you want to be a person who can talk with anyone about Jesus, these are the indispensable things. In this final section of the book, we will take time to review them all. We have spoken about techniques and methods, now we must talk more fully about a way of life, the life we must undertake if we are to be evangelists.

A Deep Interior Renewal

"The Church is an evangelizer, but she begins by being evangelized herself," Pope Paul VI wrote in *Evangelii Nuntiandi*. He continues:

She is the community of believers, the community of hope lived and communicated, the community of brotherly love, and she needs to listen unceasingly to what she must believe, to her reasons for hoping, to the new commandment of love. She is the People of God immersed in the world, and often tempted by idols, and she always needs to hear the proclamation of the 'mighty works of God' which converted her to the Lord; she always needs to be called together afresh by him and reunited. In brief, this means that she has a constant need of being evangelized, if she wishes to retain freshness, vigor, and strength in order to proclaim the gospel (15).

As we participate in the Church's evangelization, we must remain close to the Church and its sources of grace. We, ourselves, must be the ones constantly ready to repent, to listen more deeply to the Church, and to immerse ourselves in the Catholic sacramental life.

If we want to preach and teach, we must learn.

If we want to bring people to the Church for grace, we must receive the grace the Church offers.

If we want to reconcile sinners to God, we must turn from sin and be reconciled to God.

And if we want to bring people to the sacraments, we must be people *of* the sacraments.

This doesn't mean we need to be saints before we can evangelize, but it does mean we must actively live the Catholic sacramental life of charity; a life devoted to prayer, to the struggle against sin, and to the two great commandments.

Maybe you have a particular person in mind you would like to share Jesus with. Maybe you would like to be better at talking about Jesus with family and friends. Or maybe you have a general desire to be someone who is good at talking with all kinds of people about Jesus. Whatever your intentions, if you plan to share Jesus, you need to start with yourself.

Your mastery of facts is not the key.

Your grasp of the Bible is not the key.

Neither is your ability to talk about history or philosophy or even theology.

If we were intending merely to share historical information or theological points, we could easily do so from a distance, so to speak. We don't have to be personally involved with the information being communicated. But, as we have tried to make clear, evangelization is much more than just the transmission of information. It is the process of introducing a person: Jesus. And what kind of introduction can we make if our own lives are not firmly attached to his?

We must know him and live in genuine friendship with him if we are to introduce him to others.

This is the life that every single modern pope, following the teaching of the Second Vatican Counsil, has tried to call the Catholic people of this age to take up.

The bishops who gathered for that council knew they needed to help the Church find its footing in the modern world. With the Second World War behind it, with the space age upon it, and with the age of mass communication ahead of it, the world seemed filled with hope but also dangerously vulnerable to new confusions and temptations. At this crucial moment, the fathers of the council reminded Catholics that the early zeal of Christianity must be recovered for the good of the world. "This sacred synod," they said, "invites all to a deep interior renewal; so that, having a vivid awareness of their own responsibility for spreading the gospel, they may do their share in missionary work among the nations" (*Ad Gentes* 35).

It is essential to note here that the council did not just invite all the faithful to join in the work of evangelization. It invited all the faithful to "a deep interior renewal," so that we could take up the great work of evangelization.

In *Evangelii Nuntiandi*, ten years after the council, Pope Paul VI summed up the purpose of the council as making "the Church of the twentieth century ever better fitted for proclaiming the gospel to the people of the twentieth century" (2). And every subsequent pope has emphasized both the need for a renewed effort at evangelization and the need for that effort to be deeply rooted in a community committed to personal holiness.

A Church on Mission, Rooted in Christ

Although it is true that the great theme of the Church in the current age has been that all Christians must re-introduce a broken and confused world to Jesus Christ who is still Lord, it is also true that the Church has been equally insistent that true evangelization cannot happen without a personal closeness to Jesus Christ and an ever-deeper conversion to him.

Pope John Paul II devoted a great deal of his papacy to these twin calls: that the faithful must become evangelists, and that their evangelization must be rooted in their own connection to the holiness of the Church.

In his 1990 encyclical letter, *Redemptoris Missio*, after sharing his vision of a new missionary age, Pope John Paul II called the Church to renew its inner life in order to be up to

You may be the only Gospel that person will read today, and maybe the first one ever.

the task of evangelizing. "Like the apostles after Christ's Ascension," he said, "the Church must gather in the Upper Room 'together with Mary, the Mother of Jesus' (Acts 1:14), in order to pray for the Spirit and to gain strength and courage to carry out the missionary mandate. We too, like the apostles, need to be transformed and guided by the Spirit."

In his first encyclical letter, *Deus Caritas Est*, Pope Benedict XVI gave a rousing summation of the Christian life: "Being Christian is not the result of an ethical choice or a lofty idea, but the encounter with an event, a person, which gives life a new horizon and a decisive direction" (1).

In his own encyclical on evangelization, Pope Francis wrote, "A person who is not convinced, enthusiastic, certain and in love, will convince nobody. In union with Jesus, we seek what he seeks and we love what he loves" (*Evangelii Gaudium* 266-67).

On May 8, 2025, the Church received a new pope, Leo XIV, and on May 9 he gave his first homily as the Holy Father. Speaking directly to the cardinals who had just elected him, the new pope immediately took up the theme of evangelization.

"Even today," he said, "there are many settings in which the Christian faith is considered absurd, meant for the weak and unintelligent, settings where other securities are preferred, like technology, money, success, power, or pleasure."

He went on to acknowledge that "these are contexts where it is not easy to preach the gospel and bear witness to its truth, where believers are mocked, opposed, despised or at best tolerated and pitied." However, "precisely for this reason, they are the places where our missionary outreach is desperately needed." We cannot abandon the world to its loss of faith because, he said, this loss brings with it incalculable suffering: "the loss of meaning in life, the neglect of mercy, appalling violations of human dignity, the crisis of the family and so many other wounds that afflict our society."

Who can argue with this analysis? The de-Christianizing of the world has been a disaster for souls, for families, and for the whole of society. But Pope Leo did not end here. He did not stop with analysis. He reminded the cardinals that "we are called to bear witness to our joyful faith in Jesus the Savior."

No Evangelization Without Conversion

For the new pope—as for every modern pope—our era's opposition to the gospel is not a reason for the Church to turn inward or away from the world, but a reason to return to the missionary zeal of the early Church. In fact, there is a remarkable consistency in the Church's emphasis on evangelization over the last six or seven decades.

And, as did the council fathers and popes in the decades that preceded him, Pope Leo XIV took up the theme that evangelization must arise from a holy connection to the ancient Church. "It is essential," he told the cardinals, "that we too repeat, with Peter: 'You are the Christ, the Son of the living God' (Matt. 16:16). It is essential to do this, first of all, in our personal relationship with the Lord, in our commitment to a daily journey of conversion. Then, to do so as a Church, experiencing together our fidelity to the Lord and bringing the good news to all."

 Skilled witness helps, but a joyful heart is often the most convincing argument for the gospel.

The point here is that postwar teaching of the Church has involved a constant and powerful call for the whole Church to evangelize and an equally constant call for that evangelization to be nourished by lives of holiness, prayer, sacrifice, and sacraments.

An evangelist can't just be a good talker. He has to speak from the overflow of a real relationship with Christ. This means ceaseless attention to his own ongoing conversion. This means developing an interior life—a life marked by prayer, silence, Scripture, and encounter with God.

Without an interior life, evangelization becomes hollow. Instead of holy zeal, we start operating from pride, or human energy, or emotionalism. But when we build an interior life, when we stay connected to Christ through prayer and the sacraments, he speaks through us.

You can't give what you don't have, but if you truly have Christ, you have something of immeasurable value to give.

After all, "The primary reason for evangelizing is the love of Jesus which we have received, the experience of salvation which urges us to ever greater love of him. What kind of love would not feel the need to speak of the beloved, to point him out, to make him known?" (*Evangelii Gaudium* 264).

I met Jacob at a parish mission. He was enthusiastic about evangelization, always talking about the importance of sharing the gospel. But something seemed off. Tom was visibly angry with his pastor, critical of fellow parishioners, and constantly lamenting the state of the Church. Despite his zeal for evangelization, he lacked joy.

When I saw Jacob again years later, he was a different man. He told me that, during a retreat, he'd had a moment of personal breakthrough. During adoration, he recognized that although he'd been talking about Jesus to others for years, he hadn't truly surrendered to Jesus himself. He had never really repented. He'd never brought his pain and resentment to the foot of the cross.

The change was noticeable. His tone had softened. He became more patient, more humble, more loving. He didn't stop evangelizing—in fact, if anything, he became more effective at it. Now, his words had weight because they came from a heart that had itself been healed. His conversion didn't just give him a new outlook; it gave his evangelization credibility and spiritual power.

Evangelization starts in the heart. We can't give what we don't have. When we're deeply converted, striving for holiness, rooting out sin, growing in prayer, and living sacramentally, our witness becomes compelling. People can sense authenticity. The most powerful evangelists are the ones who are continually allowing Jesus to transform them. That's when people stop just hearing our words and start encountering Jesus through us.

13

Put on the Armor of God

In evangelization, it's easy to think the real work is talking to people. But the truth is that the real work is the *spiritual battle* that precedes, accompanies, and follows it.

The battle begins with our coming to know Jesus and our ongoing conversion of heart and mind. For a Catholic, this is a process that never ends in the life but only comes to completion in the next.

Sometimes people think that once they "get serious" about their faith, they're done. But we all must constantly seek deeper conversion. Deeper repentance for hidden sins. Greater love for God and neighbor. More humility, more courage, more trust.

The spiritual life is like climbing a mountain. There are always new heights. There is always more to surrender. There is always more to receive.

 The sacraments are not extras—they're the ordinary way of encountering the living Christ.

And, to our purpose: ongoing conversion *keeps your evangelization authentic*. When you know that you're still repenting, still striving, still learning, you don't preach from a pedestal. You preach as a fellow traveler, a fellow sinner who has found the mercy of God and wants to share it. Never stop converting. Never stop growing. Never stop letting Christ shape you. That's what makes your witness real—and powerful.

As with your evangelization strategy, authentic ongoing conversion requires intentional effort. It begins with spending daily time in prayer. Read and meditate on Scripture. Talk to God about your work, your struggles, your joys. Sit in silence before him and let him speak to your heart. The deeper your interior life, the more powerful your evangelization will become—even when you don't see immediate results. Because it won't just be you speaking. It will be Christ speaking through you.

Every evangelist needs help staying faithful. No one is meant to walk the spiritual life alone. That's why the Church has always encouraged spiritual direction—finding a wise, faithful guide to help you discern, grow, and stay on track.

A spiritual director can help you see patterns you might miss. A director can challenge you when you're getting lukewarm, encourage you when you're in desolation, keep your heart focused on Christ instead of the world.

You don't have to find a perfect director, just one who is faithful and prepared. Sometimes it's a priest. Sometimes it's a religious sister. Sometimes it's a layperson trained in spiritual mentorship.

The key is to find someone you trust, who is faithful to the Church, and who can guide you toward Christ. Spiritual direction isn't magic. It's humility. It's accountability. And it's a powerful help for anyone serious about evangelization.

If you can't find a good spiritual director right now, find a good confessor who knows you. Ask the Holy Spirit to lead you. Because in the battle for souls, having a guide can be the difference between perseverance and burnout.

The Armory of Evangelization

This kind of interior growth is essential because evangelization is a kind of warfare.

The Bible is clear on this. Saint Paul exhorts Christians to

> be strong in the Lord and in the strength of his might. Put on the whole armor of God, that you may be able to stand against the wiles of the devil. For we are not contending against flesh and blood, but against the principalities, against the powers, against the world rulers of this present darkness, against the spiritual hosts of wickedness in the heavenly places (Eph. 6:10-12).

When you proclaim Jesus Christ, you're challenging hell itself. You're walking onto the enemy's turf. And he will fight back.

The world will push back. Your own flesh will resist. The devil will whisper lies and stir up obstacles. That's normal. That's expected. It's not a sign you're doing something wrong—it's a sign you're doing something right.

This is why evangelists need to be spiritually fit, not just mentally ready. This is why you don't just need a message. You need armor. You need weapons. You need endurance.

Without a strong spiritual life, your evangelization will collapse under the first attack.

How do we "put on the armor of God"? What does that mean? When we look into the lives of the saints, we get our answer: by prayer and sacrifice. These are the hidden armories of evangelization.

Shortly we will talk about the various roles people take up in the work of evangelization. But no matter what our role is—whether we are talking directly with someone on the street, or setting up a table with rosaries to give out, or doing a holy hour in support of those who are out on the street—prayer and sacrifice are aways essential.

Without prayer, evangelization dries up. Without prayer, we're just shouting words into the wind. Prayer fuels the mission. Prayer softens hearts. Prayer moves the Holy Spirit to act.

Jesus didn't just tell the apostles to go. He told them to pray first. "Pray therefore the Lord of the harvest to send out laborers into his harvest" (Matt. 9:38).

Before any individual conversation, before any street event, before any mission, we should be begging God to prepare the way. Pray for divine appointments. Pray for open hearts. Pray for the words to speak. Pray for the souls you'll never even see. Because prayer isn't preparation for the battle. Prayer *is* the battle.

Along with prayer, sacrifice is our other hidden weapon. Every small act of sacrifice—every fast, every inconvenience, every silent suffering—offered in love, becomes a channel of grace. The saints understood this.

St. Thérèse of Lisieux, though she never left her convent, offered her prayers and sufferings for missionaries—and she became the patroness of missions. "Ah! it is prayer, it is sac-

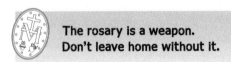

The rosary is a weapon.
Don't leave home without it.

rifice which give me all my strength," she wrote in her autobiography, *The Story of a Soul.* "These are the invincible weapons that Jesus has given me. They can touch souls much better than words, as I have very frequently experienced."

St. Francis Xavier, who baptized thousands, spent hours in prayer before setting foot on new lands. The martyrs offered their very lives so that the gospel would spread.

And us? What can we offer? How about fasting once a week for conversions? Making small daily penances: cold showers, skipped desserts, hidden acts of charity? Modern life gives us endless opportunities, as we wait in lines or get cut off in traffic, to offer these annoyances to God. We can have patience with difficult people and offer it for the salvation of souls. When we are suffering from sickness, loneliness, or setbacks, we can unite these to the cross.

When we suffer with love and offer it to God, it becomes a seed planted for eternal fruit.

Paul taught this way of sacrifice to the earliest Christian converts: "Now I rejoice in my sufferings for your sake, and in my flesh I complete what is lacking in Christ's afflictions for the sake of his body, that is, the Church" (Col. 1:24).

If we want to be fruitful evangelists, such sacrifice is not optional. It's part of the cost of love.

Most of the fruits of evangelization happen invisibly. You might never see the impact of a rosary prayed in silence. You might never see the soul rescued by your hidden fasting. You might never hear the story of someone who turned back to God because of a suffering you quietly offered. But God sees it. In fact, God multiplies it. He unites it with the suffering of his own Son, which bestows on it infinite value.

And the Kingdom grows in ways we can't even imagine. We must always remember that prayer and sacrifice are not side activities. They are the heart of evangelization.

If you want to be a powerful evangelist, you must first become a man or woman of deep prayer, and a soul willing to carry hidden crosses for the sake of others. This is how saints are made. And this is how the world is converted—one hidden prayer, one small sacrifice, one act of love at a time.

The Path of Spiritual Maturity

We've been calling evangelization a battle, and it is. When you step out to evangelize, you're not just starting a project, you're stepping onto a battlefield.

Evangelization is a direct assault against Satan's kingdom of lies, sin, and death. And he doesn't sit quietly when his territory is threatened. So, what kind of a soldier are you? How prepared are you for battle? Answering this question means not just training yourself for the fight—it means knowing your enemy.

Taking its cue from Scripture, the Church teaches that every Christian faces three enemies: the *world*, the *flesh*, and the *devil*.

In his letter to the Ephesians, the apostle Paul tells the early Christian converts that they

> once walked, following the course of this world, following the prince of the power of the air, the spirit that is now at work in the sons of disobedience. Among these we all once lived in the passions of our flesh, following the desires of body and mind, and so we were by nature children of wrath, like the rest of mankind (2:2-3).

 True witness often means embracing sacrifice and offering our own suffering for the salvation of others.

He uses the word *following* three times to describe the things that once kept the Christian separated from God—once for the world, once for the devil, and once for the passions of the flesh. To the extent that each of us is still following the world, or the devil, or the passions of the flesh, we are not following Christ.

The *world* is the culture that resists God's truth and that offers us false treasures: money, power, fame, and the like.

The *flesh* is our own fallen tendencies and weaknesses, the human inclination to prefer comfort and pleasure to sacrifice and holiness.

The *devil* is the real, personal enemy who seeks to destroy souls by drawing us away from light and peace to be caught up in darkness and pride.

These are our foes; and, if we wish to bring Christ to others, we must overcome them.

Victory belongs to Christ. But if we want to be his soldiers, we have to fight. We have to overcome those things that keep us from Christ, and the only way to do this is by the armor and weapons he provides.

Be Another Christ

The Lord asks a great deal of us because he has not just called us servants, but friends. To live in his friendship is to share in his life—a mature life of love, a life free from attachment to sin. He does not ask us to overcome the world, the flesh, and the devil because he is simply demanding, but because he wants us to share in the dignity, the glory, of his own life.

In other words, the evangelist is to be *another Christ*. It is to join him in his own proper mission—a mission for which he gave up everything. This is not an undertaking for those who refuse to struggle against sin and temptation. This is not an undertaking for those who remain spiritually immature.

Saint Peter confessed to Jesus, "You have the words of everlasting life." When we evangelize, *we have those words*, too—to the degree that we cultivate Christ's life and grace within ourselves.

It must be Christ who speaks through the evangelist, as the vine shares its own life with the branch. For two millennia, the Church has taught souls to come to God by taking on the mind of Christ. There are three stages to this journey of spiritual maturity:

We begin with the *Purgative Way*, in which we strive against serious sin.

The epistle of St. James describes this stage of the Christian life when it tells us to "draw near to God, and he will draw near to you. Cleanse your hands, you sinners, and purify your hearts, you men of double mind" (4:8). This stage involves fighting mortal sin and growing in basic virtue.

We then pass through the *Illuminative Way,* in which we begin to live in the pure light of love.

Paul describes this middle stage in Christian progress when he says that "we all, with unveiled face, beholding the glory of the Lord, are being changed into his likeness from one degree of glory to another; for this comes from the Lord who is the Spirit" (2 Cor. 3:18). This stage involves growing in deeper virtue and more purified love.

Finally, we experience the *Unitive Way,* in which we live lives of great intimacy with God.

 A genuine witness is willing to sacrifice comfort and confront suffering to share the gospel boldly.

The Lord himself describes this final stage when he assures us that "He who abides in me, and I in him, he it is that bears much fruit, for apart from me you can do nothing" (John 15:5). This stage involves deep union with God through pure charity.

Most of us spend a long time—often most of our lives—in the Purgative Way, especially when we are beginning serious apostolic work like evangelization.

In the Purgative Way, we fight against serious sin; we face fierce temptations; we often feel dryness and struggle in prayer. Our motives are still mixed—fear of hell and desire for reward are dominant.

And that's okay. The Church has always taught—and reaffirmed with clarity at the Council of Trent—that salvation is a process, a path walked in stages: from fear, through hope, to love (Decree on Justification 6).

If we have walked, and perhaps continue to walk, the Purgative Way, we are able to help others embark on this walk so that they might reach the fullness of life offered in the two ways that follow.

Through Fear to Love

Understanding the classical "three ways" of the spiritual life helps us understand our own way to God and helps us understand that our role as evangelists is often simply to help others onto the Purgative Way. We are presenting a message that, we hope, calls forth the response of repentance, faith, baptism, and a life of obedience. As we said earlier, this sometimes means being clear about sin and its consequences, lest we gut the gospel of its urgency and obscure the path that leads to life.

The *Roman Catechism*, issued after Trent, outlines the path of Christian life with precision. The first step is not something we initiate; it is God who acts first. In it, we "must proceed from the predisposing grace of God." Evangelization, then, is not about "marketing" religion or persuading by human techniques. It is about cooperating with the grace God has already begun to stir in the soul. Our task is to proclaim the truth clearly, so that those touched by grace can recognize the invitation and respond.

But as grace stirs the heart and mind to recognize God as sovereign, it is natural for fear to follow. A servile fear arises: fear of punishment, fear of hell, fear of separation from God. This fear isn't a defect in the process; it is a necessary stage. "Fear is often the beginning of conversion," says the *Roman Catechism*. "It disposes men to enter on the path of salvation." It is a wake-up call, a shaking of the soul from its slumber.

Modern ears may recoil at this. We think it's unworthy of God or beneath our dignity. But it is simply realism. Human beings, especially in our fallen state, are self-centered. We rarely seek the good for its own sake until we have been confronted by the evil we wish to escape. The Church, in its wisdom, does not ask us to stay in fear but to pass through it.

Once fear has awakened the soul, it becomes possible for hope to arise—hope that mercy is real, that forgiveness is possible, that change is attainable. From this hope, true repentance follows: sorrow for sin, hatred of past offenses, and the desire to live differently. At this point, the soul is moved not merely by self-preservation but by a growing attraction

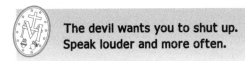
The devil wants you to shut up.
Speak louder and more often.

to God's goodness.

If we have lived the life of faith, we will have at least some recollection of these experiences, and we will have to acknowledge that moving into faith, through fear, and into hope was helpful for us. This is the path that leads to the greatest of virtues, the greatest of gifts: love.

This is the beginning of the true life of love. But it begins with fear—a truth both Scripture and lived human experience confirm. We see it even in secular society: warnings about drunk driving show crashes and consequences, not idealized visions of virtue. We understand this when promoting public safety but often forget it when promoting eternal salvation.

The evangelist who has embraced purgation as good and necessary must be willing to speak hard truths. As Jesus said, "Don't fear those who kill the body but cannot kill the soul; rather fear him who can destroy both soul and body in hell" (Matt. 10:28). Only by facing this fear can souls enter the Purgative Way—the path of purification, renunciation of sin, and growth in virtue.

To lead others onto this path is to give them a chance at the fullness of life that awaits. The purgative way, though difficult, prepares the soul for illumination—the deeper understanding of God's ways—and ultimately for union with him in love. But there is no skipping this first step. The purgative way is the narrow gate through which we must pass.

Meeting Souls Where They Are

In a case where someone already knows his sin and is weighed down by guilt, we lead into the Purgative Way by emphasizing *hope*. This was the case with a young man Steve met on the streets of Portland.

Johnny had tattoos all over his body, piercings everywhere, and a tough look that could have scared anyone off. When he approached Steve asking for a rosary, Steve asked if he was Catholic.

Johnny said, "I was baptized . . . but I'm too far gone."

When Steve asked him what would happen if he died that day, Johnny said, "I'd go to hell."

Steve didn't need to pound hell into him. Johnny already knew it in his heart.

He simply told him, "You don't have to go to hell. God loves you. You're just one good confession away."

Johnny did go to confession, and he walked out grinning and shouting, "I'm a new man!" It was simple. It was hope. And it worked.

On the other hand, sometimes Steve met people like Bobby.

Bobby was a confused Catholic. When Steve asked if he was Catholic, he said yes—but he didn't go to church, even though his brother was a priest.

Steve asked him, "Can I give you one good reason why I take my faith seriously and go to Mass?"

Bobby said, "Sure."

Steve said, "You can't get to heaven if you don't love God, right?"

"Right," Bobby said.

"And you can't love God if you don't do what he wants and avoid what he doesn't want. What if a man said he loved his wife, but never talked to her, never spent time with her, and did all the things she asked him not to do—like staying

 Mary never stops drawing souls to her son. Let her help you.

out late at the bar? Would you believe that man really loved his wife?"

Bobby thought about it, and said, "No."

Steve said, "Exactly. Same thing with God. You can say you love him, but if you're not doing his will—if you're ignoring him—your love is false. And if you have a false love, can you get to heaven?"

"No," Bobby said, starting to tear up.

"Does that concern you?"

"Yes. Absolutely," he said, now crying.

Steve told him, "It's no problem. God's mercy is waiting. Go to confession. Give up your sins. Start following God."

Bobby said, "I want to do it right now."

By God's providence, Steve knew a priest nearby. They drove to the church, and Bobby waited in line for confession. He came out beaming. He hugged Steve and said, "Thank you. You've changed my life."

The evangelist who isn't familiar with the mix of fear and hope that accompany the purgative way will struggle to help others onto it. But the evangelist who willingly walks the purgative way, and, with God's grace then moves onto the "higher" ways of illumination and union, will understand enough of the spiritual life to be honest with others.

There was no use of the word *hell* with Bobby. It was implied. You can see from this that, even without being fire-and-brimstone people, we can help others come to see the truth.

Few of the people we encounter will be saints already. We ourselves sure aren't. So, we must be realistic about the need for fear and hope, for purgation and illumination, as we strive ourselves toward and strive to help others toward ultimate union with the living God of love.

I'll never forget Martha, who was a mom of four who led a parish evangelization group. She wasn't loud or flashy, but she was deeply faithful. She had a routine: daily Mass, rosary, and Scripture every morning before the kids woke up. She said it was her "armor time."

One week, their team planned a big outreach downtown. A few days before, Martha had a nightmare about one of her kids being harmed. The next day, her car broke down. Then one of her team members called in sick. The outreach almost didn't happen.

But Martha knew the score. She said, "The enemy always hits hardest right before a breakthrough." So, she rallied the team, prayed a spiritual warfare prayer, and went anyway. That day, two people came back to the Church after decades away, and another began RCIA the following week.

Evangelization puts you on the front lines of a spiritual battle. Satan hates evangelists because we're helping to free the captives. But Scripture reminds us that we don't fight flesh and blood. We fight powers and principalities—and God equips us for the fight. Daily prayer, sacramental grace, Scripture, fasting aren't optional. They're essential equipment.

If you're going to share Jesus, expect resistance. But don't be afraid. Just stay close to the Lord, stay rooted in the Church, and keep your armor on.

14

Don't Quit!

The Catholic Church has many rules. It really does!

No, we're not talking about lots of burdensome regulations and decrees that some people think Catholics are obliged. The *rules* we are talking about are the rules—the guiding principles—of religious life!

The great monk St. Benedict wrote a rule for his monks that was meant to help them develop habits of life that made them true lovers of God and God's children. Saints Francis and Dominic, Theresa and Ignatius, and many other religious founders and leaders have written rules for their communities meant to help them live their vocations.

Benedict's rule is meant to give a pattern of life that will help a Benedictine monk. Francis's rule is meant to provide help for a very different life, the life of a poor friar. Many religious orders also offer other kinds of rules, or programs for the spiritual life, to help the laypeople in the world who associate themselves with these orders.

In its wisdom, the Church has fostered such rules because

 Start with prayer. Speak with courage. Trust the Holy Spirit.

it knows it is almost impossible to make spiritual progress without undertaking an intentional and orderly program.

So, is there such a program for the evangelist, especially the lay evangelist?

Not formally. Each evangelist will have to decide on his own "rule." But experience has given us some insights into what might make up a profitable rule for us. It includes certain essential practices every evangelist should build into his life.

1. Daily Prayer
Personal prayer every day. Morning offering. Spiritual reading. Mental prayer (talk to God honestly). Thanksgiving at the end of the day.

2. Frequent Mass and Eucharist
Daily Mass if possible. Receive the Eucharist in a state of grace. The Eucharist is food for the battle.

3. Regular Confession
At least once a month—more often if needed. Confession strengthens humility and grace. A clean soul is more powerful against the enemy.

4. Daily Rosary
The rosary is a spiritual weapon. Pray it faithfully, even when feeling spiritually dry.

5. Fasting and Sacrifice
Weekly fasting from food and drink. Small daily sacrifices, such as offering up inconveniences. Fasting strengthens the soul's will over the flesh.

6. Scripture and Spiritual Reading
Daily Scripture (even just ten minutes). Read the Gospels especially. Read good Catholic books (saints, Church Fathers, trusted teachers).

7. Eucharistic Adoration
Spend time in silence before the Lord. Let him strengthen you. Let him heal your wounds.

8. Spiritual Friendship and Accountability
Find a friend or mentor to encourage you. Spiritual direction if possible. Don't fight alone.

9. Trustful Surrender
Affirm that God is working even when you can't see it. Accept suffering and dryness with faith. Offer your work and your suffering for souls.

In Good Times and Bad

You don't need to be perfect to evangelize. But you do need to be in the fight—striving to stay faithful, striving to grow. This isn't likely to happen if you are haphazard in your approach to the spiritual life. Following your own "rule," your own pattern of practices, is essential. All such rules will include certain things in common—confession and Eucharist, prayer and community. But figuring out the specifics of how your rule will work in your own life will take trial and error, and input from mature spiritual mentors and advisors.

Even when you develop a good rule and strive to follow it diligently, one thing we can promise you is that there will be times of consolation, and there will be times of desolation.

Consolation is when prayer feels sweet, and we feel God's

presence. In this part of our spiritual life, evangelization is exciting and full of visible fruit.

Time and time again, when people start a new apostolate—or even just start practicing their Catholic faith seriously—there's a rush of zeal. They volunteer at church. They start evangelizing on the street. They read spiritual books. They can't get enough prayer.

But a few months in, a difficult reality hits. The emotions fade, and prayer feels like work. Rejection stings, and results seem invisible.

This is desolation, and when it comes, everything feels dry. God feels distant. Our efforts seem pointless. Temptation sometimes feels overwhelming.

This phenomenon isn't found just in the spiritual life. Anyone who has had a burst of enthusiasm for a new job, a new relationship, or even a new hobby can recognize the pattern of excitement at first, then the grind. The big difference is that, in the spiritual life, the stakes are eternal. So, we must be ready to meet desolation with realism and determination.

The saints teach us not to be too worried when the times of desolation come. Throughout its history, the Church has produced many spiritual geniuses, and one thing they have consistently taught is that God gives consolation to beginners to encourage them, but later he removes consolations in order to purify their love.

In his *Spiritual Exercises*, St. Ignatius of Loyola says it this way: "God withdraws his consolations not as punishment,

**Your weakness isn't a barrier—it's a vessel.
God knows how to spread his message through it.**

but to test the soul's love, to humble it, and to teach it that without him, it can do nothing."

Evangelists must understand this. When someone starts evangelizing, there's usually a burst of excitement. "This is amazing!" "I love telling people about Jesus!" "We're changing the world!"

But then the high wears off. Conversations get hard. Opposition arises. Fruits seem small. People reject the message. Even prayer feels empty.

This is desolation—and it's where many evangelists quit. They think, "Maybe I'm doing something wrong." Or worse, they think, "Maybe this isn't my calling after all."

When it comes, we must remember that desolation is part of the plan. This test of love is a necessary purifying fire. He wants to bring us to spiritual maturity in which we love him and serve him for his sake, not just because it feels good.

Because it is all part of the plan, the response to desolation is simple: *Don't quit.* As St. Paul tells us, "Fight the good fight of the faith; take hold of the eternal life to which you were called" (1 Tim. 6:12).

In evangelization, this principle applies just as much as it does in any part of the spiritual life. If you evangelize only when you feel like it, you won't evangelize for long. If you evangelize only when you see visible results, you'll give up.

Evangelization is hard. Spiritual warfare is real. Desolation is painful.

You won't always see the fruits of your labor. You won't always feel the joy. Sometimes, you will feel like a failure.

And yet Christ is victorious, and we who are other Christs are victorious with him. So, we can have confidence even when desolation comes. He has already won the war, and he invites us to share in his victory—by fighting faithfully at his side.

If you stay faithful, if you persevere, if you proclaim Christ with love and truth, you will hear the words that every one of his soldiers longs to hear: "Well done, good and faithful servant. Enter into the joy of your Master" (Matt. 25:21).

The King is worth it, and he is fighting with you.

Keep going. Keep showing up. Keep proclaiming Christ because in evangelization as in all things, faithfulness matters more than feelings.

Barbara came back to the Faith after years of sin, selfishness, and addiction. Having recommitted herself to Christ in part through the efforts of friends who evangelized her, she became convicted of a calling to be a similar instrument of grace for others.

In her efforts as an evangelist, Barbara was able to draw in a special way upon the lessons of reconciliation and perseverance she had learned in her own life. This made her, first, an effective sharer of the gospel, because her witness was inspiring and relatable to others who were entangled in sinful patterns.

And those lessons also served her in the rocky spiritual journey that evangelists face. Her life had taught her wisdom, which helped her smooth out the highs and lows, steeled her against discouragement, and ingrained in her the necessity of staying close to Christ and the vessels of grace that he provides through the Church. With all she had been through, she was not going to quit because of a few measly failures!

To come to Jesus is to be rescued from futility and to be brought into the fullness of life. Our sins, our failures, our fears, and even our deaths are not the final word so long as we remain in friendship with Jesus. Many people are stuck in their failures. Many imagine themselves to be beyond rescue, too far gone. But Jesus is the one who commanded, "Come to me, all who labor and are heavy laden, and I will give you rest" (Matt. 11:28). This is an equally crucial message for we who evangelize and those whom we evangelize.

15

Build Evangelizing Communities

We have been focusing on the life of the evangelist. If we want to share Jesus with others, then a life striving for personal holiness, a life connected to Christ through prayer, sacrifice, and the sacraments, is not optional but essential.

We can't move on from this line of thought without examining how a life of personal holiness is also a life *shared with others*. If holiness is essential to evangelization, *community* is essential as well. Because we are not just members of Christ, we are also members of one another.

Almost all of this book has been devoted to the personal efforts of each of us as individual lay evangelists. Our hope has been to help you get better at talking with others about Jesus. But we also want to make clear that if you are going to truly be a Catholic evangelist, you *need others*. At the very least, experience shows that we get better as individual evangelists the more we join with other Catholics in organized, coordinated apostolic work.

Without veering too much from our primary aim, which is to help you talk with others about the Faith in a way that is inviting and helpful, we need to turn, now, to a brief discussion of the corporate work of evangelization, because it cannot really be separated from your individual efforts.

At the beginning of this book, we pointed out that even if we don't have a personal "charism" for evangelization, we still have a personal obligation to evangelize. And we hope you have come to see that you can work on your personal skills for sharing Jesus and his Church so that you can meet this obligation.

Now, maybe you do have a personal charism for evangelizing, Maybe you are one of those people who has been given gifts suited to being at the forefront of this work. If so, then good. But don't think this charism makes you some kind of a lone gunslinger of the good news. You remain a member of a body, and you still need the other members of the body.

Alternately, maybe you don't have a particular charism for *direct* evangelization. This doesn't excuse you from trying, from doing your best. But it might mean that you have other gifts to share in support of the Church's collective evangelizing efforts.

Saint Paul is speaking to all Christians when he calls on the infant church in Rome

> to present your bodies as a living sacrifice, holy and acceptable to God, which is your spiritual worship. Don't be conformed to this world but be transformed by the renewal of your mind, that you may prove what is the will of God, what is good and acceptable and perfect (Rom. 12:1-2).

 The *whole* Church is on mission. That means you.

This is a call to personal holiness. And it is no accident that he follows this with a description of the mystical reality that each individual Christian is truly part of a body of other Christians:

> For as in one body we have many members, and all the members don't have the same function, so we, though many, are one body in Christ, and individually members one of another. Having gifts that differ according to the grace given to us, let us use them: if prophecy, in proportion to our faith; if service, in our serving; he who teaches, in his teaching; he who exhorts, in his exhortation; he who contributes, in liberality; he who gives aid, with zeal; he who does acts of mercy, with cheerfulness (vv. 4-8).

Not everyone, for example, is called to the visible front lines. And that's not a problem—that's the design. The Body of Christ has many parts, and each part has its job to do.

Evangelization isn't just about the speaker. It's about the pray-er. It's about the encourager. It's about the one who sets up the table, who drives the van, who quietly funds the mission, who offers hidden sacrifices. In God's eyes, the unseen roles are just as important as the visible ones.

If you have a heart for evangelization, but you feel like you're not the one to stand on the street corner and talk to strangers . . . good. God may be calling you to an equally powerful role behind the scenes. You still have a place. You have a mission. You are needed.

Paul uses the same "body" metaphor in his first letter to the Corinthians, where he especially encourages us not to reject our given role for another that is not given to us. "For the body does not consist of one member but of many. If the foot should say, 'Because I am not a hand, I don't belong to the body,' that would not make it any less a part of the body" (1 Cor. 12:14–15).

The Church is a *living organism*. It needs feet and hands and eyes and ears. Some are called to preach. Some are called to pray. Some are called to organize. Some are called to encourage. Some are called to finance and equip. No role is greater or lesser in God's eyes. All are essential.

Without prayer, preaching dries up. Without logistics, missions fail. Without financial support, materials don't get printed. Without encouragement, evangelists burn out. We must take care not to think of evangelization as only the visible moments. The entire body works together for the harvest.

So, in addition to the frontline evangelists, let's look at some of the other common parts of the body of evangelization.

1. Prayer Warriors

"Unless the Lord builds the house, those who build it labor in vain" (Psalm 127:1).

Prayer is the engine of evangelization. When teams are out evangelizing, prayer warriors should be interceding behind the scenes. Praying for divine appointments. Praying for open hearts. Praying for courage and wisdom for the evangelists. Offering rosaries, chaplets, holy hours. In *Redemptoris Missio*, Pope John Paul II wrote, "Prayer should accompany the journey of missionaries so that the proclamation of the word will be effective through God's grace" (78). Every mission is built on unseen prayer. Without prayer, evangelization is powerless. With prayer, hearts are opened and miracles happen.

2. Sacrificial Intercessors

"Now I rejoice in my sufferings for your sake, and in my flesh I complete what is lacking in Christ's afflictions for the sake of his body, that is, the church" (Col.1:24).

Some people are called to offer suffering for the success of evangelization: chronic illness offered for conversions, daily inconveniences embraced in union with Christ, fast days set aside for evangelization fruitfulness. We noted before that St. Thérèse of Lisieux never preached a sermon or handed out a tract, and she stayed within her little Carmelite cloister, but through her prayers and sacrifices she became the patroness of missions. The hidden cross-bearers carry enormous spiritual weight.

"The sacrifice of missionaries should be shared and accompanied by the sacrifices of all the faithful," Pope John Paul wrote in *Redemptoris Missio*. Although we can all offer such sacrifices, he made a particular call to the sick: "I therefore urge those engaged in the pastoral care of the sick to teach them about the efficacy of suffering, and to encourage them to offer their sufferings to God for missionaries. By making such an offering, the sick themselves become missionaries" (78).

3. Logistics and Hospitality Helpers

"And we exhort you, brethren, admonish the idle, encourage the fainthearted, help the weak, be patient with them all" (1 Thess. 5:14).

You can't run a good evangelization effort without someone organizing the practical details. There are tables and tents to set up, materials to be ordered. There are logistics of permits, transportation, and supplies to manage. Front-line evangelists need to eat and drink and sleep. Hospitality is evangelization, too! A bottle of water or a smile offered to a tired missionary can be the difference between perseverance and quitting.

"The mission is not accomplished through human effort alone but above all by divine grace" (*Redemptoris Missio* 36)—and grace often comes through those who support, serve, and sustain.

4. Administrative Support

"He who is greatest among you shall be your servant" (Matt. 23:11).

Behind every successful mission is someone behind a desk: sending emails, scheduling outreach events, tracking supplies, following up with contacts. All devoted to keeping the mission running smoothly.

"The whole Church is missionary, and the work of evangelization is the duty of the entire People of God" (*Redemptoris Missio* 71)

5. Financial Support

"Each one must give as he has decided in his heart, not reluctantly or under compulsion, for God loves a cheerful giver" (2 Cor. 9:7).

It's a simple reality: Evangelization costs money. Rosaries and medals. Pamphlets. Tables, tents, banners. Gas money. Event permits. People who donate generously toward these ends—often silently—are critical partners in the mission. When you fund evangelization, you share credit for its fruits.

"Those who cannot go as missionaries can still take part in the work by helping to provide for the needs of the missions, especially through spiritual and material aid" (*Redemptoris Missio* 81).

6. Community Builders and Encouragers

"Therefore encourage one another and build one another up, just as you are doing" (1 Thess. 5:11).

Some people have a special gift of bringing people together and nurturing their enthusiasm: hosting potlucks after outreaches, organizing prayer meetings, sending encouraging texts or cards, lifting up those who get discouraged. Encouragement is oxygen for evangelists. Never underestimate the power of a simple "I'm praying for you."

"Even in the most difficult situations, the missionary must not lose heart. He is an instrument of God's work and he must draw strength from the conviction that God is with him" (*Redemptoris Missio* 39).

It Takes a Community

For a Catholic, the life of faith is never just "me and Jesus." It is always a life of communion with others who are also in communion with Jesus. Around him, we live and are saved together. The evangelizing conversation, the moment when an evangelist shares the gospel with another soul, is really the tip of an iceberg. Holding that evangelist up at that moment is the great, hidden magnitude of the Church, all together. The evangelizing moment is an *ecclesial* event. It involves the whole Church.

We never fail as evangelists when we devote ourselves to the prayer and sacrifice, the organization and encouragement, the financial support, and the logistics that make it possible for evangelization to be fruitful. As Pope John Paul II affirms in *Redemptoris Missio*, "Missionary activity is a matter for all Christians, for all dioceses and parishes, Church institutions and associations" (2). If we are serious about joining in the work of evangelization, we will find our place, even if we are sick at home, even if we don't speak the language where we are, even if our gifts are hidden.

Consider just a few real-world examples of hidden evangelists.

- Years ago, on a rainy Saturday, we set up a table at a farmers' market. A woman named Mary, too shy to evangelize, insisted on coming along anyway. She quietly set up the pamphlets, arranged the rosaries, and smiled at every passerby. She never said a word to the crowd. But that table, her careful and loving hands, drew people in. Dozens of conversations happened that day because Mary made the space welcoming. And she prayed silently the whole time—a powerful hidden force behind every soul who stopped.

- On one occasion, before a major evangelization event, we organized a prayer chain. While a team of six evangelists stood at the waterfront, a group of twenty intercessors prayed non-stop in adoration chapels across the city. The fruit was incredible. Conversations were deeper. Hearts were softer. There was unusual openness and receptivity. Afterward, the evangelists said it felt like "the Holy Spirit was heavy in the air." That wasn't an accident. It was the hidden work of prayer warriors, lifting the mission on invisible wings.

- Once, when we were low on funds, a single unexpected donation paid for a thousand rosaries, twice as many pamphlets, several new banners and signs, and gas cards for transportation. That donation equipped three teams for six months of outreach—hundreds of souls impacted. The donor never stood on the street handing out a tract. But in heaven, the fruit will be credited to his account.

If you love Jesus Christ and you love souls, you have a role in evangelization. Maybe you are called to speak boldly in the streets. Maybe you are called to pray hidden in a chapel. Maybe you are called to cook meals for missionaries, or to drive them, or to pay for their rosaries. None of these roles are second class. The front-line evangelist cannot do his work without the prayer warrior, the organizer, the donor, the encourager—all of whom are his partners on the battlefield, helping Jesus to conquer hearts for his kingdom.

Never believe the lie that you have nothing to contribute. Your "yes"—even hidden and quiet—shakes hell and builds heaven. There's a place for you in the mission of evangelization. Maybe on the street. Maybe on your knees. Maybe at the kitchen table. Maybe behind a keyboard. Wherever God calls you, answer boldly. The harvest is great. The workers are few. And the battle for souls is raging. Together—front-liners and hidden warriors alike—we can storm the gates of hell and bring home the lost. This is the time. This is the fight. And you have a role in it. Take your place. And don't look back.

 Start with love, end with Christ, and trust everything in between to God.

The Jesus we share, if he is to be the true, historical Jesus, cannot be disconnected from his own Church. His Church is, in a mysterious way, his own body, and we cannot have a full relationship with him apart from it.

In his first letter to St. Timothy, for example, the apostle Paul writes a great deal about the importance of the Church, saying that his whole purpose in writing the letter is so that "you may know how one ought to behave in the household of God, which is the church of the living God, the pillar and bulwark of the truth. Great indeed, we confess, is the mystery of our religion" (1 Tim. 3:15-16).

Thus, from the very first, evangelization has been an invitation to know Jesus and to share life with him within the Church he founded (Matt. 16:18). Though evangelization may pass through many stages, in the end, this is what we hope, in every case, to share. This is why we evangelize believers as well as unbelievers: so that all can come to the fullness of what Christ offers them.

Go and Make Disciples

At the Second Vatican Council, the council fathers taught emphatically that "the whole Church is missionary, and the work of evangelization is a basic duty of the People of God" (*Ad Gentes* 35).

The Church "exists in order to evangelize," Pope Paul VI wrote in *Evangelii Nuntiandi*, "in order to preach and teach, to be the channel of the gift of grace, to reconcile sinners with God, and to perpetuate Christ's sacrifice in the Mass" (14).

In *Redemptoris Missio,* Pope John Paul II shared his vision for the coming age of the Church. "I see the dawning of a new missionary age," he wrote, "which will become a radiant day bearing an abundant harvest, if all Christians, and missionaries and young churches in particular, respond with generosity and holiness to the calls and challenges of our time" (92).

And, as we have already shared, in his very first homily as pope, Leo XIV spoke of the difficulty of evangelizing in the modern world, and of the suffering that comes from the absence of faith.

We live in a time of great confusion, and in such times, it is understandable when people seek comfort and safety. But

Jesus is the only hope for this broken world. Proclaim to it his holy name.

the Church is called to do more than hide away. To be Christian is to be called to love others with the kind of love that shines a light in darkness and brings clarity amidst confusion.

When people are starving for truth, we are called to proclaim boldly the saving truth of Jesus Christ.

When people are starving for love, we are called to share the love of Jesus Christ.

When people are dying for hope, we are called to offer the hope we have received in Jesus Christ.

If we have real love for the people of these lost and confused times, we must get better at speaking about Jesus, at sharing him even when we don't really feel like it. You already know this. It's why you have this book in your hands. And because you have come to the mature desire to share Jesus, you really can talk about him with anyone.

It's time for all Catholics to take up the call with love, with courage, and with perseverance.

We aren't just selling a positive lifestyle or promoting good values. We are proclaiming objective, eternal truth: God exists. He created us for himself. Sin has separated us from him. Hell is real. Heaven is real. Jesus Christ is the only Savior of the world. Repentance and faith are necessary for salvation.

If we leave out the bad news of sin, judgment, and hell, then the good news—mercy, salvation, eternal life—makes no sense. We must proclaim the full gospel, not a watered-down, feel-good message. And we must do it clearly, lovingly, and without apology.

"For I am not ashamed of the gospel; it is the power of God for salvation to everyone who believes" (Rom. 1:16).

If we offer merely love without truth, we commit a betrayal. But we must also constantly remember that truth without love is a hammer. True evangelization is always rooted in love.

Evangelization isn't about winning arguments or scoring points. It's about loving souls—loving them enough to tell them the truth, to pray for them, to walk with them. We listen to people's stories. We meet them where they are. We speak truth into their lives with compassion, not arrogance. We offer them hope, not condemnation.

Love means patience. Love means mercy. Love means refusing to give up on someone even when they reject us. When people know that we truly love them—not as projects, but as children of God—their hearts open.

Evangelization must always flow from love. Because love is what moved Christ to the cross. And love is what will move souls to him.

Never Forget, the Mission Is Simple

Finally, evangelization demands faithfulness. Remember: we are not responsible for results! We are responsible for our faithful response to Christ's call.

If you preach the gospel and no one listens, you have still succeeded. If you plant seeds and never see the harvest, you have still done your duty. Evangelization is about obedience, not outcomes. God alone sees the heart. God alone brings the growth.

"So neither he who plants nor he who waters is anything, but only God who gives the growth" (1 Cor. 3:7).

You may never see the fruits of your efforts on this side of eternity. But in heaven, you will see the souls that were touched because you were faithful. Stay faithful. Keep

Our willingness to endure suffering with faith can be the most powerful form of witness to Christ's love.

showing up. Keep proclaiming Christ, whether it's convenient or not, whether you feel successful or not. Faithfulness is success in the eyes of God.

The mission is simple: proclaim Jesus Christ —boldly, humbly, and lovingly. Not ourselves. Not our politics. Not our opinions. Jesus Christ—crucified, risen, and reigning.

Speak his name. Tell his story. Offer his mercy. Invite people into his Church.

The world needs saints—men and women on fire with the love of Christ, willing to proclaim him boldly and joyfully. Be one of them.

If you evangelize seriously, you will suffer. People will misunderstand you. Family members will criticize you. Friends will drift away. You will experience dryness, darkness, desolation. Don't be surprised. Don't be discouraged. The cross is part of the mission.

But so is the Resurrection. You will also experience indescribable joy: the joy of seeing a soul turn back to God. The joy of seeing fear conquered by love. The joy of knowing you fought for souls and stood with Christ. And even when you see no visible results, trust this: God is working in ways you cannot see. No act of evangelization is ever wasted.

Say Yes

Every Catholic is called, and every Catholic is needed. You don't have to be a professional missionary. You don't have to have all the answers. You just have to say "yes."

Say yes to proclaiming Christ in your family, at your job, in your neighborhood. Say yes to being a light in a dark world. Say yes to stepping out in faith even when you feel weak. Say yes to being part of God's great rescue mission for souls.

The world needs you. The Church needs you. Jesus Christ is calling you. Say "yes" to loving people enough to tell them the full truth about Jesus Christ—in joy, in charity, in faithfulness—and trusting God with the rest.

You were made for this. You were baptized for this. You were confirmed for this. You were saved for this. Go, and make disciples of all nations.

Go, and bring the light of Christ into the darkness. Go, and proclaim the only name by which we are saved: Jesus Christ.

The world is waiting. The time is now. And Christ is with you always, even to the end of the age.

An Invitation to St. Paul Street Evangelization

St. Paul Street Evangelization (SPSE) is a grassroots Catholic evangelization organization founded to train and equip ordinary Catholics to share the gospel in public places. SPSE operates on the belief that evangelization is most effective when done in community. This approach reflects the biblical model established by Jesus himself, who sent his disciples out two by two. Today, SPSE evangelists can be found on street corners, at festivals, and in city centers across the country, joyfully sharing the message of Jesus Christ.

Joining SPSE is simple. Those interested can visit the website to find a local team or start one themselves. New evangelists receive training, materials, and ongoing support. By becoming part of an SPSE team, members gain a spiritual family committed to the mission of evangelization.

When we founded St. Paul Street Evangelization, we built it around this simple truth: Evangelization is easier, more joyful, and more fruitful when done together. SPSE is far more than just an organization; it's a family of evangelists.

SPSE is made up of men and women who love Jesus and want to share him. And we do it side by side, two-by-two, just like the Lord taught us.

When Jesus sent out his first evangelists, he didn't send them alone. "After this the Lord appointed seventy-two others, and sent them on ahead of him two by two into every town and place where he himself was about to go" (Luke 10:1).

Jesus, who could have equipped each person individually, chose to send them out in pairs. There's a reason for that. Evangelization can feel intimidating. You're stepping out, facing strangers, sharing your faith. It can seem overwhelming at first.

But the truth is—it's not as hard as people think once they start. And when you have someone with you, it becomes not just easier—it becomes joyful. Community isn't just a bonus for evangelization. It's a strategy. It's a protection. It's a spiritual lifeline.

And if you want to evangelize effectively, joyfully, and for the long haul—you need to know: you were never meant to go it alone—even though sometimes you will.

From the very beginning of the Church, evangelists moved in groups or pairs: Peter and John together in Acts 3; Paul and Barnabas sent out by the Holy Spirit in Acts 13; Paul traveling later with Silas, Timothy, and Luke. The apostles gathered in groups to pray, strategize, and support each other.

Of course, this pattern isn't absolute. Sometimes even when alone we are called to evangelize, and there are lots of important moments of solo evangelization in the Bible: for example, Paul at the Areopagus (Acts 17), standing alone before the philosophers of Athens, or Philip and the Ethiopian eunuch (Acts 8), one-on-one in the desert. Sometimes, by God's providence, you find yourself witnessing alone. Sometimes the moment demands a personal encounter that no team can replace.

Both are good. Both are necessary. Both are part of the missionary spirit of the Church. But for public outreach, for growth, for training, and for long-term endurance—community is indispensable. "Two are better than one, because they have a good reward for their labor. For if they fall, one will lift up his fellow" (Eccles. 4:9–10).

To have a community, whether it is a single friend or a large circle of evangelists, makes each person's efforts easier, stronger, and more fruitful.

At every SPSE event:

- We evangelize in teams, not alone.
- We pray together before going out.
- We support each other during conversations.
- We encourage each other when things get tough.
- We hand out rosaries, Miraculous Medals, and good Catholic literature.
- We offer prayer.
- We proclaim the name of Jesus with love and courage.

And when one person gets discouraged, the other lifts them up. When someone feels stuck and the right words don't come, their partner is there to step in and help. When one gets timid, the other says, "Come on, we made a commitment. Let's go."

And after the outreach, we rejoice together—whether we spoke to a hundred people or just one soul.

This is the beauty of evangelization in community. It's not complicated. It's not high-pressure. It's joyful. It's faithful. And it's sustainable—because no one is fighting alone.

If you've never done public evangelization before, joining an SPSE team is one of the best ways to get started. You'll find brothers and sisters who will walk with you, pray with you, and help you grow in boldness and charity. Street evangelization isn't about arguing. It's about loving. And when you do it side-by-side with others—it becomes one of the greatest joys of your life. St. Paul Street Evangelization exists to make that possible.

Even secular studies show that people who have accountability partners are 80 percent more likely to reach their goals. How much more in the work of saving souls?

For the evangelist to build evangelizing habits, stay faithful, and reach more people, community is critical.

Find your team. Find your family. And then go—together—into the streets, into the world, into the heart of the battle. Then, when needed—you'll be ready to stand alone, boldly—knowing Christ stands with you.

The world is waiting. And you are not alone.

In Christ,
Steve Dawson

About the Authors

Steve Dawson is founder of St. Paul Street Evangelization, a Catholic apostolate dedicated to proclaiming the gospel in the public square. After a radical conversion, Steve has dedicated his life to the Church's reason for existence: the salvation of souls. He lives in Michigan with his wife and best friend, Maria, and their six children.

Cy Kellett is the host of the award-winning radio show *Catholic Answers Live* and the author of *A Teacher of Strange Things: Who Jesus Was, What He Taught, and Why People Still Follow Him*.